This book has been inspired by many years of designing natural landscapes, working with my hands in the soil in gardens throughout California and observing how natural systems thrive. More than a how-to manual on gardening, permaculture or design, these pages are a reflection of how I weave gardening, permaculture and design processes in to the fabric of my life based on tools, understandings, teachings and principles that I have learned and integrated over the years. Maybe you will find yourself in these pages, or perhaps inspiration and a jumping off point as you embark on your own journey to create and cultivate a garden for your dreams to thrive in the landscape of your life.

ISBN: 978-0-578-79464-8

I dedicate this book to my north star
and guiding light, Vianna.

With gratitude to my wonderful partner, friends, family, and mentors along the way who have inspired me to keep reaching, stretching, learning and discovering the magnanimous nature of life.

Thank you to Larry Santoyo, Toby Hemenway, Scott PIttman, Josiah Clark, Paul O'Donnell, Giselle O'Donnell and Beau Bonneau - some of my first teachers and fellow earth stewards.

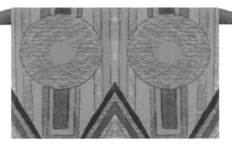

Thank you to Dr. Gochette, Thomas Olona, Eilish Nagle and my mentors in Peru for helping me evolve beyond myself and love with a deeper vibrato.

Notable and deep gratitude to Suzanne Strong for her artistry and sublime photography of our gardens captured here in this book. Thank you as well to Jennifer Toole, Siouxzen Kang, Jocelyn Miller and Nicol Ragland for their photographic contributions.

Wholehearted appreciation and respect to Carly Jo Carson for her inspired illustrations and layout and to Joanna Pawlowska for editorial insight and guidance. Deep thanks, as well, to Scott Robson, Kate Bower, Alma Tetto, Ellie Victoria, Mike Townsend, Robert Gillman, Bill Vetrop, Jenny Wapner, Allison Luterman, Rico Epifanio and our Viola Gardens crew of gardeners and clients for their contributions and support to this creative endeavor.

"The miracle is in the eyes that see, not what is seen."

-Ino Moxo

Introduction
The Ethics of Growing a Garden

Introduction

The Ethics
of Growing
a Garden

YOUR LIFE IS A GARDEN. You are a garden. Everything is possible through design.

Many years spent in the garden have shown me over and over how life grows, moves, changes and evolves in time. Hands to the ground and head below my heart, gardening has lifted me up and guided me through many difficult moments in my life, revealing an extraordinary path to healing and empowerment.

This book is a collection of lessons and insights I've drawn from working with nature as a designer and gardener over the years. I hope that by sharing these seeds of insight, I might help you discover the power, strength, tenderness, and compassion within your own garden — and within your own life. May you find that the natural principles of garden design, which encourage abundance and growth, can reveal a path for your practice and your own sense of personal empowerment throughout the many seasons of your life.

A garden is a place of possibility. Life constantly changes, moves, grows, decays, and becomes in the garden. I am in constant awe of the web of relationships that connects plants, birds, butterflies, and even mountains beyond a garden's fence line. All part of a shared ecosystem — a co-evolving and endless experience of relationships in time and space.

A good garden design never forces itself onto the landscape. Instead, it yields itself to the principles that govern nature to arrive at design solutions that respect and encourage healthy relationships between plants, wildlife, and people, inspiring beauty and cultivating bounty.

Similarly, the design principles which govern life systems in the natural world offer us a map as to how we, too, might use these natural processes of design as tools for growth in our own lives. A holistic approach to designing our relationships and communities demands that we learn to follow nature's lead, that we pay attention to the patterns that govern natural systems, and that we develop a sympathetic commitment to embody this wisdom in our everyday lives.

At its core, "Permaculture design" is, simply, relationship. Its fundamental aim is to understand how all elements function in relation to all other elements in a given system. Everything exists in relationship with everything else.

I've committed many years to learning how to understand nature — why and how it does what it does — and then applying those patterns to design models for personal growth, community resilience, and for cultivating better relationships between people and the world around us. It's a marvelous practice. I am endlessly enchanted by the natural world. The more I learn and observe, the more I realize how much more there is to learn and observe. There is so much to celebrate.

I've come to understand: We are nature. Our bodies, our blood, our DNA. We are made of the very same elements that make up the stars in distant galaxies, that make up the nourishing plants that heal us, that make up the water that sustains us. We are made of the same stuff as the flowers that provide beauty, food, and abundance. To respect any one part of the system means we must respect all parts that make the system whole.

As Permaculture designers, we make three simple commitments:

1. To care for the earth
2. To care for people
3. To extend all energy and resources towards the above ends

These commitments exist in relationship to each other. To nurture yourself and the landscape of your heart is to nurture the planet and the landscape of your life. To nurture the planet is to nurture all life, which in turn includes you.

Learning to apply the wisdom of the garden to the whole of my life has transformed how I perceive everything around me. Becoming aware of the life-sustaining gifts of water, wind, sunshine, earth, and air fills me with so much gratitude. This practice of gratitude, in turn, yields greater awareness. Which only leads to more gratitude. I am in awe of how much had to happen — so many diverse systems and functions had to align perfectly — for us to be here now, alive on this planet. For anyone who, like me, has felt the sting of isolation, worry, doubt, fear or despair, may this remind you: we have enough, we are enough, we belong.

Permaculture design teaches us to care. To care for the planet, care for each other, and care for ourselves. These seem like revolutionary concepts in a world that profits from our human divisiveness and self-indulgent banality. We forget that together we will always be stronger than we are alone. That we exist in relationship with everything on this planet. The more we can learn to connect to ourselves, to our bodies, to our natural resources, and to each other, the stronger, more resilient, and more sustainable our world can become.

There must be trust for the circle to work.

We must organize around a shared value system rooted in a simple truth: humans need this earth and all of its systems of life to sustain our life systems. Our survival as a species depends on our willingness and ability to work with nature, not against it. This truth exists outside of ideology or religion. It's a truth that unites us all. We need each other. And we must remember that self-sufficiency is not the same as self reliance. No one is coming to save us. We are all here with the blessed opportunity to contribute and offer what we can to the whole for the betterment of the whole. Diversity is key and active participation is required by all.

Separating ourselves from the wisdom of nature and our part in her natural order is a recipe for disaster. We digitize our experiences and forget what it feels like to put our hands on the ground and touch the earth. We distance ourselves from our instinctual drives. We lack the knowledge to support ourselves in basic ways, like growing food, harvesting water, and cultivating peaceful relationships. We've forgotten that differences strengthen systems because they offer the diversity that yields resilience. Differences are part of a holistic perspective that takes into account the earth and all of her people.

This principle holds true in our individual lives: We mature into the people we are meant to become, not in spite of our problems, but because of them. We find grace as we work through adversity with generosity. And we embody grace when we extend beyond ourselves, all the while, rooted, like trees, to our core self.

Natural design teaches us that true power and strength comes from extending beyond ourselves. We grow beyond ourselves when we think beyond ourselves.

Every parent — and every ecosystem — knows this deeply and intuitively. The loving act of nurturing someone or something generates a humbling sense of power, clarity, and ease. It forges deeper connections with ourselves, with each other, and with the planet. It shines light on what is essential.

It takes courage to be what the world needs. It takes courage to cultivate peace when the world is not peaceful. It takes courage to choose a fresh alternative over panic and consider how we might better care for ourselves. It's a lifelong practice that can begin in the gardens we tend.

To nurture the earth, to nurture our relationships with ourselves and others, is to nurture the gardens of our lives. There is no separation. There is only balance. The path to peace within is the same as the path to peace without. The two are forever intertwined.

The world has never been a place. It has always been a process. Natural design is a work of art in motion across space and time. Each choice and action creates the conditions for what is to come next. Nothing happens in a freeze-frame.

Understanding how natural systems function and flourish, and applying this understanding in our lives, offers us the opportunity to design abundant, beautiful and forgiving gardens for our dreams, in both the landscape of our lives, our relationships, and within the landscape of our hearts.

Onward.

"Genesis"

Life begins here.

Ears buzzing with the evening sounds of crickets, night songs that begin under starry Amazon skies, telling a story that's been told since the beginning of time, telling a story that already knows itself, that begins in the air, that exists to create itself infinitely because it can, expressing untold and unimaginable beauties. Some may call it possibility.

Here where the stars still shine, remnants of another time. A time when oro-tongas and dancing lizards dreamed, dreaming endlessly and without tiring, the dance between opposite ends of day and night, the same, dreaming a never-before-seen love.

Dreaming a creation story where even the sounds -- and especially the sounds -- join together in perfect symmetry, neither good nor bad. Just is. The sounds of the jungle, of our cities, our days and nights come together to sing a song of harmony, if we are listening. The sounds sing to balance each other. A most supreme love-making, so delicious and so divine that light and color somehow find a way to transfer their until-then never- before- seen knowledge into mass and matter. So that we, then, might come together. So that we might once again, like never before, hold hands and look out at a river moving in time. A pure expression of the simple awareness that to be here, together, to look out at a river moving in time, is a supreme gift. It is here where two become infinite. All one. It might begin upon these shores of creation, where sorcerers and whales, ants and owls, friends, lovers and unborn babies conspire at night, silently, without light,

To participate in a ceremony that is protected by an ancient knowledge. A wisdom superior to human intelligence. A caring so supreme it tells a story that no botanist and only a dreamer, only a lover, fully understands.

It's impossible to listen to all the sounds at once. It's impossible to remember all the creatures in the sky and land and desert and forest and sea in one moment. It's impossible to sing a song today that is yet to be born tomorrow.

From the air we arrive here, and all we have are the stories we tell. But from the air, in the great revolution of this awakening, is love. And beauty.

Balance and harmony. In this moment, seconds and centuries.

Tonight I can hear my future singing to me, dreaming me into creation. Taking shape to live the life only I can live. To share what passes through my formless shape so that love and that divine essence is recycled back to the heart from which it came. A love I am over and over borrowing to give back. My ayumpari, this type of love.

All that ever was and all that will ever be is held in these moments. Always moving and changing in space and time so that the cosmic nature of our star-like hearts can dance and kiss and laugh, simply, because we can.

Zone
Zero

HUMANS ARE COMPLEX AND LAYERED CREATURES. We can come to understand ourselves through a core tenant of Permaculture design: an environment as a series of Zones. Imagine that "Zone Zero" is our baseline orientation within our lives and on the planet. For many, this can be a connection to the divine self or a deeper aspect of consciousness. As a root concept, this connection with a higher level of consciousness can direct the physical experiences we create and manifest in life. What's going on inside sets the stage for what is happening in our physical space. Our thoughts, our feelings, and our affinities inspire the beliefs, actions, and lifestyles we choose. Our Zone Zero is our orientation, which leads us closer to what and who we love.

They say it is possible to love anyone as long as there is the right relationship of time and space between two people. In the garden, every element, every function, every choice is relational. Time and space — and their relevance and importance — often guide how systems are built. Permaculture Zones are a dynamic management tool and organizing force used to prioritize relationships in time and space given energy required and attention needed. The closer an element is to the center of human life, the more attention it can receive and the more that affects the available time, energy and health so that all efforts within a system can thrive.

Permaculture is a system of design that maps our experience inside ourselves using principles which we have observed over millennia to work outside in the natural world to cultivate balance, regeneration, health, and abundance.

In Permaculture there are infrastructures and invisible structures. Infrastructures are tangible systems of design that we create to keep a society engaged and functioning. Invisible structures constitute all the social systems, including personal relationships, that govern and create our society. The same natural patterns that govern and inform life in nature work when designing our social constructs, for example our health, justice, education, legal, transportation, psychosocial and economic systems. Equally we can use these system designs to lift and vivify our personal lives.

What might it look like to consider appropriating and prioritizing your life in relationship to what matters most to you, much like a garden, for the benefit of the whole of your life? What would it look like to appropriate and prioritize your own life and wellbeing? As we deepen our understanding of the delicate interconnection between the relationships in our lives, including with ourselves, we create conditions for balance and regeneration in our lives at large.

In the landscape I often begin by asking how a client will be using the space. It is the relationship between the people and the space that determines placement and design.

Who are you, where are you, why are you, and how are you in time and in space, today? What inspires and excites you most to act with intention as a creative co-designers here on this planet?

Understanding what is most important to you — what makes you feel most alive and aligned — is the first step towards mapping out the Zones of your life. And like in Permaculture Design, this map holds wisdom for how to care for and cultivate each Zone …and so how to fortify the whole. Naturally, this can feel very overwhelming! A good place to start is by establishing your personal inventory through a series of questions. The list can be as simple or extensive as you choose but some questions you might begin asking when establishing your personal inventory could be:

- What is the overall feeling you have when you think of your life and relationships you share? Which aspects of your life mean the most to you?

- Do you believe in a Divine presence or a higher power in your life — and how does that presence affect your experience in life?

- How do you express self-love and self care?

- What is your relationship with time in your life — your daily routine, the pace of your day, the rhythm?

- How do you relate to your family and what is your level of intimacy with the ones you love most?

- Does your house and the land you live on encourage a sense of 'home', of belonging?

- What is your relationship with your body, with the foods you eat, and how you feel in your body?

- Do you feel a connection with your community and if so, why?

- What is your relationship with your purpose, your passion, and the work you do in the world? Is it integrated in your life and what kind of meaning does it create for you?

We can begin to ask ourselves questions that reveal truthfully how we relate to all aspects of our lives and how the various parts of our lives relate to each other. The more fully we understand our relationship to ourselves and the various parts of our lives — and much like elements in a design, consider variances in what we do, where, when, how, and why — we cultivate more alignment and flow. When we are aligned to the truth of who we are in our souls, we will always be in the right place at the right time. We will always see the silver lining, the ever unfolding opportunities for growth and renewal.

In my experience, I resonate with a sense of divine consciousness in life. For me, Zone Zero is my spiritual compass and where I find the deepest connection and consequential framework for my life. This includes my personal practice, like meditation, music or prayer, as well as my physical practice, yoga or hiking, or a practice of writing and reading. Staying aligned within myself brings greater awareness, presence and engagement to all other areas of my life. Zone One is my family, namely my daughter. Loving her gives meaning and direction to my other important relationships. Family, for me, is love and at the core of my matrix of personal design. Tending my most intimate familial relationships inspires and directs all aspects of my life. Zone Two is my sense of place and purpose in the world, which is greatly inspired by my work. Nurturing my relationship with work is integral to making sure that I am continually evolving and able to bring more to it. This means maintaining a holistic practice within the context of my design work from drafting to installation, as well as feeding myself with knowledge, learning, and inspiration by spending time in nature. Similarly, I find solace and grounding in my home space by creating beauty and engagement within my surroundings. A home is more than a habitat — and a passion and purpose vastly different than a job. Zone Three is my community, it's where I live, and it nurtures a sense of belonging and place. Like ripples in a pond, I prioritize the right relation with what feeds the whole, right relationship with a higher power, the earth, my family, my purpose, my home and community because I have learned that this sense of orientation, when properly designed in my body, mind and soul, feeds the whole.

In a personal context, we can use this same technique of pattern literacy by understanding how to use the appropriation of Zones in relationship to ourselves, our homes, our sense of place and space in life, our families, our communities, and our world.

In a world that profits from our ambivalence, it is radical to consider yourself, to be nice to yourself, to listen to what excites you most, what fills your being with passion and purpose, and then to follow the path of least resistance towards your true joy, trusting that doors will open even if the path is not fully revealed.

Using natural design in the landscape, we often use Zones in the context of the home, the needs of the people and the land. For example, we start with the object of our intention. Let's say, in a physical context, a home. The home, a place and a container for the people. A place that provides nourishment and warmth, comfort and stability. A home is not just a house, but a place where we are rooted in time and in space with ourselves and perhaps with other people. A home, "Zone Zero," is our point of departure in this context.

If the intention is to build a garden that nourishes the people in the home with food and sustenance, in "Zone One" you would place things like herbs, vegetables, and flowers for pollinators, and you would want to plant them close to the kitchen to be used by the people in the kitchen. You would want to understand who is in the home and what they like to eat, what colors and smells uplift them, what to plant that will be used and harvested, cherished and enjoyed. You create first the relationship between the core components of function and form.

You then radiate out to "Zone Two." Here, perhaps you have chickens, or your compost pile, your rainwater harvesting set up. "Zone Three" might be fruit trees, cover crops. "Zone Four," honey bees, seedlings, a green-

house. And on and on, depending on the nature of your design and the intention of the relationships between elements that you desire to create.

It doesn't take long for elements within a system to respond to the health of their environments. Gut reactions or instincts occur in real time and are immediate. In a garden, bio-indicators arise and let you know whether a plant is getting too much or too little water, too much or too little light. Similarly, emotions are useful indicators, and offer biofeedback signals along the way that help us understand how our bodies are experiencing the world and people around us, and the next right action needed in a given situation. They are the little blinking lights that go off inside and help us decide whether to move left or right, to trust, to jump, to stay, to speak, or not. Our intuition is a byproduct and integration of the emotional responses and gut reactions which our bodies indicate in response to certain experiences. Anaïs Nin wrote that we see things not as they are but as we are. In Permaculture, we strive to maintain a reasonable grasp of the obvious. To see through our own unique lens what is apparent, what is occurring in present time, right here and right now, and to listen to, respect and respond appropriately to the indicators present.

I see this in the early days of a relationship. Our bodies and minds integrate who this new lover is — and we recognize, on the spot, the ways we can relate to each other, or not. People show us who they are from the first moments we interact. Then, as we form attachments and feelings arise, particularly in romantic relationships, we squint our eyes and tilt our heads, attempting to convert other people to our experience. When the illusions fade and we see them once more for who they truly are, tragic-comic stumblers like ourselves, we blame them for being who they showed us they were in the beginning. This creates conditions for more feelings of various shades, keeping us stuck in a self-perpetuating cycle of illusion. We forget our natural instincts and the ability to engage our intuition at any moment. We share this means for survival with all living beings.

As we come to fully trust ourselves and our intuition, we can stand fearlessly in the truth of who we are — and trust that we know who others are, too. They have shown us themselves, after all. With radical acceptance of what is, we allow relationships to naturally form with those whom we share an affinity with for one reason or another. Our natural intelligence becomes our guide and begins to supersede outside opinions.

Trust your feelings. Identify the friendlies. Deepen those relationships first.

As we strengthen the relationships within our own being and the intimate relationships that bring ease, we broaden our perspective and appreciate the inherent possibility of relating with the world that exists around us. The world is full of infinitely glorious creations and combinations far beyond what any one person can conceive.

The point is not to dumb down our emotional thermometers so to make it palatable to live in a world with the heartless, or to anesthetize our instincts to get along with more people, or the wrong people for us. The point is to experience the full spectrum of being in relationship with ourselves and our divine sense of self, and to develop more friendliness and kindness towards ourselves first, Zone Zero, so that we can deepen our capacity to engage in healthy relations in our world as active, generous participants. So we can become Earth Stewards.

I believe our capacity for joy and love are proportional to our capacity to hold our grief and pain with a tender and loving heart. I've learned this working with plants over many years and have seen how regenerative and forgiving a garden can be. Rather than avoiding the full spectrum of feeling, we practice so that we are able to hold it all, balancing the duality of life, allowing ecological processes inside to function and flourish, including the wisdom of our hearts.

All growth creates discomfort. These edge experiences teach us how to work with who we are, wherever we are, so that we can have a more direct and authentic experience with ourselves, with the divine, with the people in our lives and the world around us. The more patience and kindness we learn to exact towards ourselves, the more capable we become of experiencing patient and kind relationships with others. The more compassion we cultivate towards ourselves, the more compassion and understanding we can cultivate in the world around us. The more comfortable we learn to be in our skin, the more we allow others around us to be more comfortable in their own skin. As such, our relationships deepen. Permaculture design is the relationship — and when our relationships are healthy and functioning, we can cultivate sustainable and regenerative dynamics in our person, our families, and in our communities.

In the spirit of Permaculture, we are here to discover how to cultivate sustainable relationships, accepting that there will always be differences. By focusing on the strength of places where we overlap with others, we find that balance and peace is possible. Growth and evolution as a species are then possible. Every person on the planet is here to create the life they wish to live. Every person on the planet is here with the capacity to dream

and translate those dreams into reality. As we become more tolerant and aware of how these natural life systems connect us, how they work and our place in the circle, we become more accepting of diversity and differences, understanding that the health of a system is often generated because of our differences, not in spite of them. We create a world where all of us can live the lives we wish for.

Borrowing the concept of Zones from ecological design, we learn to prioritize relationships with ourselves, our children, our partners, immediate family, friends, community, city and onwards out as the framework for how we wish to exist in relation to each of these. As we integrate these principles, we can come up with viable solutions. There's no right or wrong. No blueprint for the unique experience that best fits our personal needs. We feed the relationships that excite us. As in any design, once the vision is clear, we can then create a plan of action.

We can use this principle of Zones to organize and map the design of our lives, using the filters and teachings discussed in this book, to increase the effectiveness of our efforts. By making intentional decisions about where we want to put our energy, we can nurture our gardens to manifest dreams into reality.

"*There is a vitality, a life force, and energy and a quickening and it is translated through you in to action. And because there is only one of you in all of time, this expression is unique. If you block it, it will not exist. It is not your responsibility to determine how good it is or how valuable or how it compares with other expressions. It is your responsibility to keep it yours. Clearly and directly. To keep the channel open*".

- Martha Graham

2

Pattern Literacy

WE LIVE IN A WORLD OF PATTERNS. They are everywhere. Everything, including us, is shaped by a tessellation of events. Everything is defined, described and developed by the space around it. Think about the shapes, sizes and sounds of the world around us. All of nature — human beings, animals, birds, insects, water, wind, and mycelium — seek patterns. Nature constantly looks for ways to rearrange itself to increase efficiency, create relationships, maximize yield and exist in sustainable and balanced dynamics. Human beings are no exception when it comes to how we govern our societies, or how we build our marriages. We seek patterns.

My mentor, teacher and dear friend, Larry Santoyo, always reminds me to "seek to maintain a reasonable grasp of the obvious." We seek to observe, without judgment or assumption, what is occurring and why, understanding that natural succession is how the world evolves. Everything that occurs creates the conditions for the next thing to happen. We can predict the future by staying keenly aware of the present.

The moment we are clear inside, everything outside unfolds. When we have a clear desire, we create a pattern of thought which inspires the physical expression of those thoughts and creates our experience. When we cultivate a pattern of thought, positive and useful, or the opposite, we cultivate patterns of feeling which influence our behavior and the behavior of others which we are then attuned to. What are your patterns of thought and can you follow the through line from thought to feeling to behavior to experience in your life? Are you happy with what you do for work? Do your relationships inspire you and uplift your days? Does your lifestyle bring health and vibrancy to your life? Does your work, your relationships, your lifestyle encourage you to share that love with others? How do the patterns you create bring you closer to or further from the life you want?

Learning to understand the language of plants, of gardens and of natural systems is not as complex as we've been made to believe. There are not an infinite number of patterns in the world, but a finite, measurable and, once seen, easily recognizable series of formulas, habits, and patterns that govern all life. Consider that all life forms are "eco-phenotypic," meaning they are shaped and sized by the world around them. The palm tree growing on the coast has formed in shape to bend with the tireless coastal winds, fronds already frayed. A flatfish is round and flat, evolving in high pressure, low density conditions at the bottom of the sea.

Our lives, our bodies as well, are a summation of the shapes, sizes, sounds and experiences of the world we live in. People touch our lives and create an impact, becoming the foil for a change in who we are and how we see the world. We are a summation of our experiences, and we move in patterns. Human patterns are based on beliefs. Our lives are shaped by our beliefs as well as the beliefs of our parents, the beliefs of the society of which we are part. And our beliefs create conditions for our thoughts and feelings which create the conditions for the choices, actions and behaviors which create our experience.

All ecosystems the world over share a core set of patterns and principles that govern their capacity to naturally sustain and flourish. There are patterns at play on multiple levels at all moments in the natural world. When I design a garden, I look first for patterns and use them to cultivate relationships in the landscape, including between the people and the garden. These patterns ultimately inform the detailed design decisions to come. Learning to recognize patterns in nature and in our lives as we would a garden allows us to step back and obtain a perspective of the bigger picture and our place in it. Predictable patterns emerge. And they emerge over and over and over throughout systems. From this holistic perspective we become able to better understand how things interconnect.

This same, great teacher of mine, Larry Santoyo, also said to me, "Consider the possibility that not everyone wants to be like you. The whole world does not need to change for us to be sustainable." It is not until we change our minds, beliefs and behavior that real transformation, from the individual to the family to the society, becomes viable and real.

The zen of strategizing recognizes the patterns at play — from the smallest details of our infrastructure to the watershed of which our business, our life and our relationships are just one part.

The Classroom

a blank wall

a blank canvas

empty chairs of possibility

a garden of dreams, tended with the sweat and tears of this one salty life.

these two hands.

the announcement of hope the acknowledgment of fear

a giving garden of possibility. an opening.

a chance.

a second chance.

the lives that fill these chairs, each rooted with their own story, their own history,

their own grief, their own celebrated victory,

and the relief,

the belief

that it only takes that

to believe.

to believe in your life. to believe in yourself.

that's power.

a calling.

a calling to try.

a calling to help.

a calling to try and help change something for the better. a calling to change for the better.

or let it die.

the courage it takes to break your own heart.

to change and rearrange this whole life for love. to live for love in the face of betrayal

and still, to live for love.

and in love, the courage it takes to stand still. to stay.

true gardeners know how to arrive at solutions without imposing their will.

broken, tired, head in hands.

you are welcomed back in to the circle.

a flower cannot bloom with just heat.

the parts contribute to the whole, each element necessary and unfamiliar.

clumsy, we learn to come together.

we learn to surrender.

engulfed, we dance with a knowing that is bigger than either you or me.

with a knowing we are part of something bigger than you or me.

there is a great strength in the differences between us.

you move, i will follow,

you pull, i will surrender

i will trust you to cherish my one precious heart. my one precious life.

the alchemy of relating, changing, mixing, fading, burning believing.

orange to blue and blue to brown.

the possibility.

create what you can believe in.

the dance ensues.

the dance becomes the hero and you, a dancer.

the wild courage it takes to let it be.

there must be some correlated emptying of all you have learned until this moment

to sit still in an empty chair and allow your mind

your heart

your body to open

to the full possibility

of what you can do with your one, little life.

if you can't go on as before

then certainly, you have no choice but to go on as you never have.

3

Trust in Our Soft Skin

IF THERE IS ONE THING I KNOW FOR SURE AFTER MANY YEARS OF TENDING EARTH, it is that choosing to love — ourselves and others — may be the greatest success of all. It is perhaps one of the most important choices we can make as humans and earth stewards.

How do we learn to trust ourselves so we can trust others? How do we learn to trust our place in the world? How do we come to know forgiveness? Where is the heart of compassion? As we cultivate our inner garden, developing tolerance and understanding within, we deepen our capacity to experience greater tolerance and understanding outside of ourselves. If we hope to live in a world in which we can build communal design systems and work together to cultivate peace, with each other and with this nourishing planet, it must start within each of us.

Imagine living your life for just one day with no resistance at all. No matter how you judged or interpreted what came your way, you would remain open and allow yourself to build the capacity within to tolerate what came up. You would sit with discomfort long enough to find space around it and allow it to transform. You would be as nature is: There is no part of nature that resists any part of itself. A tree doesn't wish it was a fish. A fish doesn't live its life longing to be a rock. If there is a lack of health or flow in a system there is equally an opportunity to repair what is out of balance. The natural world will expend energies using principles of Permaculture to improve the relationship between components to better the whole system. When we are in direct resistance to our experiences, we block the opportunity to grow. It's a tough lesson, but with compassion, humility, courage and strength we create more space for ourselves and others — and thus build trust in the bigger arc of our lives and relationships.

I learned about resistance, and ultimately surrender, firsthand while going through my divorce. I unintentionally lost 20 pounds during the process. There was just so much that I found hard to swallow. There was so much being revealed: big lessons that I wasn't prepared to learn and realizations about the darker side of human nature that changed me forever. After 11 months of marriage, and with a small 2-year-old, we were suddenly in the throes of a very challenging and high-conflict separation. My love for my daughter, Vianna, became my lighthouse — and I held on tight, forcing myself to be stronger than I thought I could be, for her. I knew then that I had to take time and really dig deep to understand what in me created the conditions for this cycle of abuse to germinate. Otherwise I would undoubtedly repeat the pattern with someone else. And likely so would my child. So I learned to double down on what I loved most. I worm-holed in, turning over rocks and stones, following clues and learning to stay with what was breaking me. Learning to look more closely at what was right in front of me that I didn't want to see. Learning to sit with my fear and all the emotional reactions I was experiencing so I could begin to understand and finally swallow what I thought I could not. I learned that it was that pain, that exact heartbreak, that loss of naivety, that would come to equally nourish me in many new ways. It transformed my heart and taught me the beauty of self-love, the gift of compassion, and the true meaning of forgiveness. It taught me to trust in my soft skin.

Where had I gotten lost? I believe most of us suffer from a too-quick tendency to sabotage our own self-worth. We judge ourselves, we criticize ourselves, we compare ourselves to others. We hold ourselves to an impossible mark and then, when we fall short, we judge ourselves for not living up to the mark we established in the first place. We live out of time with ourselves, our experiences, and the world around us — and then play this out in our relationships and social constructs. It takes a brave heart to sit squarely in the center of what we find uncomfortable and to offer ourselves the love, understanding, acceptance, and compassion we are desperately seeking from the world around us.

Forgiveness — self-forgiveness — is an art and a practice. Love, including and especially self-love, is a messy and complicated dance that often requires courage and patience.

The work is not to live a perfectly-ordered and tempered life within some paradigm that you, or someone else, invented. The real work of evolution is learning to live authentically, truthfully, moment by moment. With courage we allow the mystery of vulnerability and the intrigue of curiosity to open our hearts so we can have a direct experience with life, all of it. Like an alchemist, we turn over and follow each experience through to the end so we can recycle the love we borrow and offer it back.

I realize now that so much of what I went through — what we all go through — comes from stories passed down from our ancestors. Lessons that someone learned somewhere along the line, that became our stories.

If there is to be any hope for our future generations, it must start within each one of us.

Be curious and honest: What is the story you are passing along?

We need to engage our souls in an active way, as participants here on this stony planet, to breathe life into new stories that propel us towards what we wish to create, so that we can reveal our true, natural beauty and experience the magnificence of our one, singular life.

What inner shift needs to happen to reclaim the natural, wild self and allow that part of our being to find its place in this modern world? Obsessed with appearances, we project onto the world an image of who we think we're supposed to be: strong, oiled-up replicas of who we actually are. We stifle and suppress what feeds us. We reject what makes us unique and gentle. We seek to correct our bent branches and push down the ways in which our hearts move, to make it palatable to live in a world with the heartless. We learn over and over to disassociate from the pain and trauma of being sensitive creatures in a dynamic world, and in doing so we cut ourselves off from the natural, free-flowing life-force that sustains us and all life on this planet. Our grief is the counterpart to what we praise, and both comprise the integral parts of living in this world alongside the wholehearted.

Nothing in the natural world disappears. Everything moves from one shape to the next, from one way of existing to the next. Life is constantly changing, rearranging, to breed more life. Our lives are no exception.

We will keep relearning the lessons until they are learned. There is no sidestepping the healing. If you are to live among the wholehearted and thrive, not just exist, your participation is required. If global peace is ever to become a world phe-nomenon, your participation is required. You must be willing to let your soft skin be exposed to the cold air in whatever ways are needed, and for however long, in order to metabolize your experiences, integrate them so you can hold more for the world, and the people you love.

The subtle, vulnerable, and life-giving aspects of our tender, soft skin, our gentle beings, must be given the opportunity to touch the breaking light and grow, much like a seedling, to become what we are meant to be. Shaped and sized by the world in all ways.

The path is never straight but rather often twisted and narrow. We honor each of these natural life cycles when we allow ourselves to feel them authentically and without judgment, treat them with respect and compassion, and move through the process with dignity. We honor what we love and how we love when we allow the love we lose to nourish us and breathe new life back into our bodies, hearts and souls. Grief is a natural response to missing what we hold dear. Healthy expression of emotion through the body allows for a deeper experience of the beauty of being truly alive. This practice allows us to bow down to what has caused us pain and find a way to honor and lift up what sustains us. It allows us to become embodied, fully alive beings in a world that we have the impossible and fortunate opportunity to be a part of.

It takes a lot of courage to step into the shadows of who we think we are and shine a light on what shames us, makes us feel vulnerable, exposed. In essence, to love what makes us human. In my experience, shining a light in the dark has been a way of deepening my true knowing of who I am within, of getting to know the light inside me. This is what encourages me to rise and meet life on life's terms and recognize the light in others. To be ultimately committed to Love in itself as a way of life.

Choosing love over fear. Choosing authenticity, choosing self-acceptance, choosing forgiveness. Choosing to live on the growing edge of who you are, and all that is possible in who you are, is a way of giving back, a simple way of recognizing the divine in you and the divine in others. When we live in alignment in this way with ourselves and with each other, we can feel our alignment with the planet, our kinship with the natural world and natural ways. Working together to employ better systems of design to save and steward this planet must come from a place of love, a place of connection, and not from fear.

Learn to swallow what you think you cannot. Learn to sequester the wisdom of your choices, good and bad, and recycle that energy as you move forward. Turn up the volume on what you love and let it shine a light in the darkness. Life is a joyful experience, with so much beauty and richness. Live from your bones. Trust in your soft skin.

she fell in love with the moon

her already shadowy bones exposed to
the night from behind
a cage around her heart
her skin peeled back to expose the heart
still pumping blood from within
 in the wake of his December.
dim, but pumping.
no one could tell the difference but she was cold
she was see-through
she was fragile from the leaving
especially from behind.
her loved ones, her child, they could all see her bones.
she was told to eat.
but what they would never know is the energy, the
strength it took to find
a way to
swallow
what was being revealed.
it was all very hard to swallow.
and so
the room changed
no longer the same room now
her skeleton keeping her form, pulling her upright
through the world
but
her fleshy substance erased
From her heart her gaze
night after night
the moon returning to hold space with her until one day
she looked up
and she felt love
and in the moons reflection, her eyes open, her heart
lifting, her own majesty
returning this love she had once borrowed, the same
love she had once sought from her pale winter lovers
who could not grasp her power
and even if they could, weren't up for the challenge of
meeting her here
at night
naked and exposed
recognizing her heart while gazing in her eyes

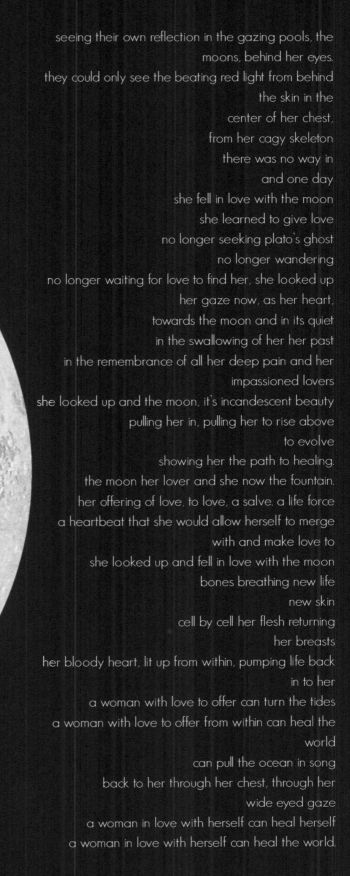

seeing their own reflection in the gazing pools, the
moons, behind her eyes.
they could only see the beating red light from behind
the skin in the
center of her chest,
from her cagy skeleton
there was no way in
and one day
she fell in love with the moon
she learned to give love
no longer seeking plato's ghost
no longer wandering
no longer waiting for love to find her, she looked up
her gaze now, as her heart,
towards the moon and in its quiet
in the swallowing of her her past
in the remembrance of all her deep pain and her
impassioned lovers
she looked up and the moon, it's incandescent beauty
pulling her in, pulling her to rise above
to evolve
showing her the path to healing.
the moon her lover and she now the fountain.
her offering of love, to love, a salve. a life force
a heartbeat that she would allow herself to merge
with and make love to
she looked up and fell in love with the moon
bones breathing new life
new skin
cell by cell her flesh returning
her breasts
her bloody heart, lit up from within, pumping life back
in to her
a woman with love to offer can turn the tides
a woman with love to offer from within can heal the
world
can pull the ocean in song
back to her through her chest, through her
wide eyed gaze
a woman in love with herself can heal herself
a woman in love with herself can heal the world.

(Inspired by Liz Huston's painting
"She Fell in Love with the Moon")

*"The most common way people give
up their power is by thinking they
don't have any."*

— Alice Walker

4

Principles of
Permaculture and You

IT TAKES COURAGE TO SHOW UP FOR LIFE AND RISE, ESPECIALLY WHEN CHALLENGED. It takes courage to live from the bones and follow what excites you deeply, in your core. It takes courage to accept the power you have to change your life, to discipline your thinking and support your thoughts in action, and then to consider how your actions affect and assist the lives of others. Once we find our courage, principles of Permaculture can illuminate where to go and how to think beyond ourselves.

Remember, we grow beyond ourselves when we can think beyond ourselves.

Think of daily life in your community. If you were to consider what you need, what you have to give, what resources you have to share, what skills you can offer in support of what moves you most, you would find the opportunity to develop new connections with people in your life, closing loopholes while deepening relational systems of exchange. Consider that it takes 50 to 100 people to provide everything that 50 to 100 people need. Everyone can bring something unique to the table. As we think outside of the box the whole picture shifts.

What we give, we get back.

It takes a person living in their power to recognize the effect they have on the world they live in and to live generously. It takes power to embody our values and take action in our lives to create the world we want to live within.

In Permaculture design, we often speak to core principles that summarize the highest generalizations for how life functions in all natural systems on earth. These principles serve as guidelines and, ultimately, filters, which, when used, direct our design most effectively. As natural designers we learn that by returning to these principles we do not need to impose designs, but are guided through natural succession to arrive at designs that make sense. As my friend and mentor Larry Santoyo teaches: "We do not 'do' Permaculture, we use Permaculture in what we do."

In essence, Permaculture has been used and applied around the globe for thousands of years. Bill Mollison, one of the co-authors of the language we know today as "Permaculture", defined six core principles that we can apply in any design, from our infrastructures to our invisible structures (community, economy, education, art, livelihood, etc).

These six core tenets of Permaculture are:

• Multiple Functions for Every Element

• Multiple Elements within Single Functions

• Recycling the Flow of Energy

• Stacking in Space and Time

• Biological Resources

• Relative Location

When applied to our everyday lives, these principles are very effective in conceptualizing our purpose and bringing it to life in the world. As always, we create with the intent of being beneficial to the planet and to other people, including ourselves. As we explore these principles in this book, I invite you to consider these time-tested strategies that govern all life-sustaining systems on the planet. Consider how they might help illuminate a path of healing and deeper connection to the landscape within and in doing so, allow us to connect more deeply to the world outside of ourselves.

When we are rooted to a sense of self within that is connected to something bigger, we can realize our full potential and allow ourselves to express what it is we are here to express. We can heal ourselves and others. As we learn to integrate patterns of natural design within our lives and live in deeper alignment with the natural world, we can work together to build and develop systems that support the health of our planet, our communities, our families, and ourselves. Everything is possible through design.

For me, the inspiration to do this work, both the internal work and the practice of garden design, comes from a deep calling within to heal and connect to that divinity in myself through nature. Living in service to plants and natural systems has inspired me to find ways of helping people discover how wondrous, magnanimous, and intelligent these life systems are and how healing it is to connect to them. Working with plants, observing the natural world, and creating gardens is endlessly fascinating and inspiring. The more I connect through nature to myself, the deeper and more authentic the connection within me is to other people — which in turn inspires me to help others find the same connection to their gardens and the natural world along the way.

If we can find ways to see, consistently, beyond our own limited and self-absorbed perspectives and recognize how truly interconnected we are to this glorious planet, and all of its life systems, we can then create the self-reliant and interconnected relationships we need to build a sustainable infrastructure, in our lives and within our communities, regardless of differences. Where there is an edge there is possibility. Where there is difference, where there is struggle, where is discomfort, there is a growing edge of possibility for what can heal and transform.

I can only imagine how our world might change if we were able, all of us, politicians and philosophers, mothers and engineers, to consider the picture outside the frame. To consider our garden beyond the confines of our fence line. To consider that each resource we enjoy, without exclusion, comes from one place and is going to another. And then to consider that the wellbeing of one element in any system benefits the wellbeing of the whole. Without exclusion.

The world is not utopian. In fact the balance of nature exists because of the duality present in all life systems. The world is not good or bad. It is both at once. And even with all the human and fallible and natural and imperfect ways in which we interact with each other and the planet, there is hope in the knowing that none of it happens in a freeze-frame. Each experience creates the conditions for the next thing to happen. And every person, every single component is integral to the whole.

Nature is not a philosophy. It is science and an art. We are blessed to enjoy the bounty and abundance of our planet by virtue of life systems that have been at play for millennia. It's non-interpretable. It's the way it is. Nothing alive lives in a bubble. No life system, no person, no plant, no animal. We need one another. To act with integrity and offer support breeds potential. To receive support breeds possibility. Imagine embodying your full power and living your thoughts into action because living in alignment with the best of who you are feels good. Imagine the power you can wield.

Permaculture design is powerful and it feels good. Permaculture is a design system based on observing nature and developing a set of principles that are in harmony with the natural world, allowing ecological functions to occur while still keeping a place for human beings within it. We strive to design our lives and life-systems in harmony with what this intelligent planet has shown us works. In doing so we allow ecosystems to function, rather than trying to convert ecosystems to the human experience. Very simply, through the practice of better understanding how to recognize the intelligence of natural patterning, we learn how to work with nature and not against it. As we resolve a state of peace within, we learn to live in the flow and are then able to work with our own nature and not against it. And equally, with each other, and not against each other.

Multiple Functions for
Every Element

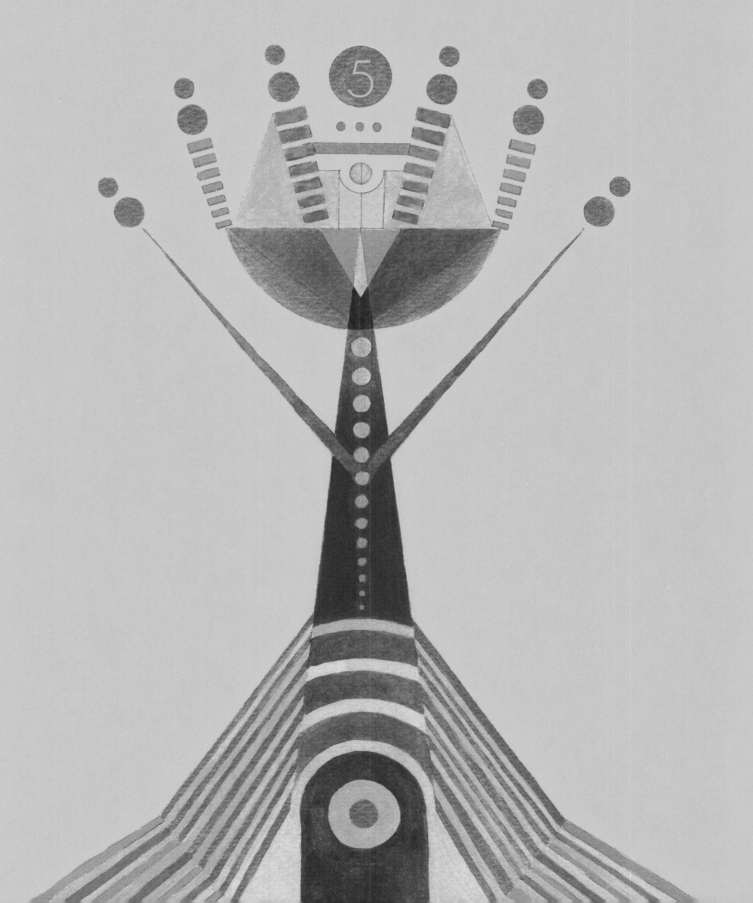

EACH ELEMENT IN A NATURAL SYSTEM SERVES MULTIPLE FUNCTIONS. A lemon tree on the north side of a house is evergreen and drought-tolerant, it creates shade, provides food and blossoms for pollinators, smells good and has solid root systems to help in erosion control. One tree provides a multitude of benefits. As we begin to consider our lives through the same lens, we begin to see how each part of our lives contributes to the overall design of our lives and the lives of others. Who we are, what we enjoy in life, what we "do" for work in the world, our relationships with our families and beloveds, our homes, where we live, how we like to live — all of these aspects of our personal experience create the web that makes up our lives. These aspects of our lives are connected. The more each part contributes to the whole, the healthier the whole is.

How many functions does each singular aspect of our lives serve in meeting the optimum vision for the overall arc of life we desire? By starting with a core understanding of what we intend and who we intrinsically are, we begin to discover that certain elements inherently contain several functions. We are able to understand what is working and understand the multiple functions each aspect of our lives serves to benefit the whole infrastructure of our lives. We can learn to cultivate better relationships between those aspects of our lives by choosing which components we want to nurture most in the garden of our experience, components that feed us on multiple levels. As we begin to clarify what is serving us best, most efficiently and effectively, we create the conditions for abundance, peace, health, and greater happiness.

No one part of our lives exists out of relation with the others. Our bodies, our minds and our souls are deeply intertwined. Some say we lose our mind and come to our senses. Learning to balance the interplay between these parts of me has taught me much over the years. I knew early on that I needed to build a life that was creative, grounded, intelligent, physical as much as mental, and that I needed a sense of freedom and autonomy to thrive and maintain equilibrium. I was never going to have a cookie-cutter life and I never wanted one. There was "no one-size fits all" major I could get behind in college or career I could pursue that encompassed all of me. So I created a career, built a business and a life around what worked for me, what I loved most. I considered all of me in order to figure out what I needed to thrive, the shadow and the light, the strong and the sensitive all a part of this design. I built multiple functions amongst singular elements such that the infrastructure of my life and the inner world of my being might all find harmony.

I have always had passion for the wild and creative muse. Growing up in a suburb just outside of New York City, I would steal out to look up at stars in the dark of the night while my mom and sister were sleeping. Still the distant hum of life and orange hue of lights in the sky, I would ponder what other worlds existed, the incredible density of living dwarfed by the abstract knowing that somehow, in some way, I, too, was made of star stuff. These moments were golden, personal and quiet, as if the stars themselves were speaking to just me and reminding me that no matter what I was living through, no matter how disconnected or alone I would often feel, that there was a place for me in the circle. That the light deep inside my being, no matter how small or untouched it felt when I was scared or lonely, was real and a part of something bigger and more vast than any sadness or anxiety. I would remind myself that what was going on at that time in my life and within my family — which left me feeling bewildered and disconnected a lot of the time — was a narrative and at any moment I was free to rewrite the world I wanted to live in.

Every person has a story. I'm no exception. I also know what I've lived through, how it's shaped the person I am, and the choices I have made in my life. I lived through some very difficult experiences in my childhood. On my quest for inner peace, I've spent many years unwrapping these memories and working through their hold on my mind and within my body, wanting that my scars might help and heal, myself and maybe others. It's been a long journey of self-acceptance and self-love as I have learned to reclaim disassociated parts of myself that were lost in trauma.

Music has always been an ally and has helped me heal. It was music that was my first love. Learning to sing and play the piano as a little kid was how I first began, in my own small way, to transmute pain and emotion into beauty. My piano teacher was from Guyana and didn't speak English so I had to learn to play very intuitively, focusing less on a grasp of theory and more on the music I felt. The piano gave the quiet parts of my heart a voice. Singing drew up emotions from the depths of my soul and set them free, creating shapes and rhythms, discovering expression through vibration. I would sing and play and a scream would turn into a song or a sob would turn into a serenade and it brought me peace. When I surrendered to the music and let it come through me, I found I could lift myself and other people to higher ground.

Or even just level ground. Some days that was enough.

My heightened sensitivity and deep, inquisitive disposition taught me at a young age that I needed a daily practice to engage with my creative muse less I would sink quickly into depression. I practiced piano and sang until I was in a trance. Day and night. I would listen to cassette tapes of Whitney Houston and sing along until I could sing with her in key. I started keeping a personal journal when I was about 8 years old. It was one of those kids' journals with the little key. I wrote every night before bed. A little prayer in my own way. Every morning I would seek poems, quotes, songs that would inspire my day. That made me feel good and lifted me up.

I started going to Alateen, which is Al-Anon for teens, when I was 11 years old. I remember walking into a beautiful church by a duck pond and looking up to see an old man wearing green and red plaid pants and black-rimmed glasses beelining for me as I stood in the door afraid to move. Without skipping a beat he said, "Coming in or out?" This same man, 75 years old, would turn to me a year later after reading my poetry and say, "Jess, you have a choice in this life. You can feed your fear and your pain, or you can feed the joy, the gratitude and the light in your soul. Write from that place".

So I did. And writing from that place helped me clarify important questions — questions I would learn to work through in the soil.

How do we deal with disappointment or heartbreak?

How do we metabolize the harsher aspects of living within our own hearts to create more peace in our lives and world?

What is the narrative we choose to follow and live by?

What do you need to experience an integrated way of being in the world and feel peace with how you live?

For years, these questions have pulled me to the garden. Hands in the earth, pulling weeds, planting seeds, pruning, singing a song, writing a letter in my head, saying a prayer, listening, feeling, sensing, imagining. Touching the ground beneath my feet with my own two hands, knees on the ground, head below heart and heart above head, I discovered another practice that became integral to my well being.

My creativity and passions would lead me to canyons and forests and deserts and oceans and, in some small way, I would connect, then, to something divine, something bigger than me. In turn, connecting with the divine was the doorway to my creative practice.

When I arrived in Ithaca, NY, where I went to college, I recall getting lost in the moonlight, walking by the lake with a friend on one of my first starry, late-summer nights. I remember the initial fear of being immersed in such a wild silence, such a deeply dark and all-encompassing beauty. Up until that moment I had never been so removed from people, city hums, planes, cars and all the busy-ness that keeps people from standing still and listening, especially growing up in New York City. In the years to come, a great knot slowly began to unwind as I spent more time in those Gorges throughout Ithaca, writing papers, reading Carl Sagan or Alice Walker or Adrienne Rich or Jorie Graham, Rumi, Hafiz, Salman Rushdie, Tom Robbins, science journals, philosophical texts on Sufis or Taoists or Buddhists or studying installation artists or philosophers. That natural quiet became nourishment and I found a small voice inside that over the years I befriended and learned to trust. All the while listening to the incessant arc of these tremendous waterfalls hitting stone, shaping the slate with each drop, together a power and a force.

I knew then I could never live out of relationship with the natural world. It was only in surrendering to the details and nuance of what was there, the beauty and intricacy, that I discovered in my young life again, and more deeply this time, that I was connected, the same, a part of this world and at that, connected to something Divine. Those starry, starry nights staring up at the sky as a child carrying me forward as I became a young woman, set out to create a life of my own. Being immersed in nature once again reminded me that somehow, amidst all the heartbreak and folly, I belonged. This was family.

They say a bird can't sing in a thicket of thorns. Each one of us is a unique impression of the splendor of our own natural design. Each one of us holds seeds which if nurtured, if fed, if listened to and honored as sacred, will touch this world in a way that only our one life can.

As we begin to make an inventory list of our lives, from where we live, to how we live, what we eat, who we spend time with, how much money we make, how fulfilled we are personally, spiritually, emotionally, we can then begin to notice which components, if nurtured, might satisfy several functions in our lives and, in fact, support and nurture the other components creating an integrated and regenerative inner and outer world. It's possible that we can experience peace and harmony in all aspects of our life by aligning ourselves within and seeking relationships between the various components of our life that bring us fulfillment.

The point is not to disguise or dismiss or deny aspects of our lives or our person that are complicated and cause us pain, but to find a way to accept and integrate ALL of who we are. To find a way to integrate all of our life experiences and the intrinsic characteristics that make us who we are. To find functional connections between the various aspects of our inner lives which inform and direct our joy and experiences outside of ourselves.

The world is an expression of the seen and unseen. As we explore ways to build relationships between the various components of who we are and aspects of our lifestyle, the whole becomes integrated and sustainable. So that together, all of who we are and how we move through the world, uniquely, can be better understood. As we build a regenerative web of inner relationships that are aligned, we find we can use our grief, our failures, or our shame to fuel our joy, our successes and our own personal empowerment. As holistic and integrated people we use the principles of Permaculture design as a guide to actualize whatever it is that we wish to achieve.

This is similarly how we build guilds in our communities, with other people. Everything has a place and everyone finds a place.

As we begin to identify and work with who we are in this way, identifying the multiple elements of our being which best support the intentions we have for how we wish to feel as we move through the world, what we wish to do with our lives, how we wish to contribute, we can then spiral out and begin to apply these same core principles in our communities, our schools, our political and legal policies with other people and forge regenerative social structures.

The spirit of this Permaculture principle then is to form functional connections between various aspects of a system. A whole-hearted and honest inventory is how we begin.

As we begin to consider our lives through the same lens, we begin to see how each part of our lives contributes to the overall design of our lives and the lives of others.

6

Where Do You Get Your Water?

I MOVED TO CALIFORNIA FROM NEW YORK ONE MONTH AFTER GRADUATING FROM COLLEGE. For three years, I worked as a producer on several documentary films. The projects were interesting, but the hours were long, I was inside all day, and while creatively stimulated at times, my body — which was used to dance and yoga after spending years in a B.F.A. conservatory — felt atrophied. As much as I loved the heart of documentary film work and felt it was important to be learning and sharing these stories, a life in the film industry was not for me.

I needed a job. A simple job that could help me support myself while I acclimated to life on the West Coast, 3000 miles away from all of my family and friends at the time. I also needed one that would allow my spirit to feel alive and my body and being to feel balanced. I recall a quiet moment in my back garden in Fairfax, CA. It was the spring of 2000. I had just enough money to put gas in my car and was feeling lost and homesick. I asked myself very simply: "Jess, what do you want to do? Just for money. Not a 'career.' Just a job to support yourself here in California until you figure out the next step." The answer came purely and quietly. All I heard from the little voice inside me was "I want to work with plants." I wanted to be close to nature and I wanted to get paid for it. I found the closest plant nursery to my house, which happened to be a California native plant nursery. I walked in and met a man who would become one of my greatest teachers and dearest friends in life, Paul O'Donnell. He asked me if I had experience with horticulture or ecology. Nope. He then asked me if I had experience with retail. Nope. Then he asked me where I was from. New York. And so was he. And that was that. I left my number and went home.

The next morning he called. The nursery manager had quit and I was offered a job, starting at $10/hour. I had found a teacher — and my boss had found a student.

Throughout the years I spent working there I was asked to identify every native plant on the land and at the nursery, many of which were propagated locally. I needed to understand the soil conditions that were necessary for each plant to thrive and organic remedies for a host of garden problems. I was always encouraged to be creative. I loved to sing when I watered the plants each morning, so that's how I started each day. I began to feel a kinship with the plants at the nursery and the birds, insects and other life systems that they created conditions for. I came to look forward to the early rise and getting back to the nursery to check on them, to get to know them more and observe how they responded to different exposure, to help nurture them. Caring for them gave my life a very simple meaning. I marveled at how different plants would go dormant in the winter only to reemerge in spring. Because I tended the soil all winter long, they came back with more glory than the year before. I learned over time that from the roots we grow strong. And that sometimes, some plants need better light, better soil, to grow more abundantly. To grow healthy.

I found inspiration in learning about how plants grow and ecosystems flourish which resonated with me on a deep, soulful level and inspired me to want to learn more about plants and ecology. It was the same connection I found years prior in the Gorges of Ithaca. I felt humbled, daily, as I came to understand the poetry of the living world and my place in it. My turbulent childhood and all the subsequent experiences up until that point — the poetry, the meditation, the yoga, the dance, all I had learned about art, music, theater and film — began to find context within a wider lens. The more I understood how plants grow, why they grow in some conditions and not in others, which plants like to grow near other plants and which do not, the more my life and who I am began to make sense, take root. I began to listen to the creative spirit inside from the wellspring of that inspired learning, in that special little spot on a corner in west Marin County. I would paint a sign near one pocket of the nursery, near a stained glass door and an old bathtub in the shade garden, which I would convert into a planter and botanical display of hanging ferns and delicately placed

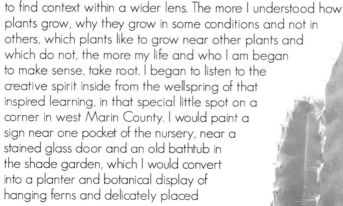

natives, a rich array of color, texture and form. The sign I would paint recalled Joseph Campbell's sage advice in big, bold letters: "Follow Your Bliss".

That little pocket of the nursery was where our customers would often congregate. Over time we added a table and chairs and hosted classes on organic gardening, vegetable gardening, habitat restoration. We hosted poetry events and friends would come and play music. While tending the nursery, my coworkers and I would read Thoreau and encyclopedias on plant species, we would experiment with worm bins and compost piles, talk about ecology, ornithology, the people we loved, our families. We got excited each year during the season's salmon run, and would enjoy fresh-caught fish from the rivers after work for weeks, in the nursery with a little campfire with friends. I was one of two women who worked in the field doing habitat restoration amidst a group of stellar men. I was encouraged to learn how to do everything the men did. Or at least what my body would allow me to do. I was encouraged to get strong and use my core. I was taught to build and install French drains, irrigation systems, amend soil, weed, prune, and plant. I learned how to operate a chainsaw. On 9/11, when my family was unreachable, most having jobs in the financial district in Manhattan, my mentor brought me to a property at the top of Mt. Tamalpais. He taught me how to dig holes in clay soil so that we could plant sizable fruit trees in this open expanse, at the top of a mountain. All the while, the sky was silent and so were we. There were no planes and no words. Just the sound of two shovels touching earth.

Sometimes the undoing, the release, the quiet and the surrender are the talisman needed to light the way forward.

My time at the nursery was profound and set the stage for all that was to unfold. The year was 2001. The world changed forever in an instant. I spent another year or so tending seeds and gardening. Not ready to settle in this perfect little mountain town in Marin at such a young age and enamored with the horizon lines, I decided to take a job in San Francisco, using my "college education." I would move on to work at a casting agency for film and TV, heading up an on-camera acting school and building the foundation for a digital casting platform which would revolutionize casting called Casting Networks, a.k.a. LA Casting. As fate would have it, I found myself working for another wonderful man, another mentor. Another friend for life. Beau Bonneau. Beau saw something in me that I couldn't see in myself at that time. He took a chance on me, believed in me and began to teach me about business systems, bookkeeping, finance and the crazy world of movies, commercials and casting. Beau taught me how to run a business.

When I moved to Los Angeles in December 2005, I remained at the casting agency for as long as I could. Once again, my body was stiff from working in an office every day, inside at another computer. As much as I wanted to stay, I knew I had to move on … again. Even with the promise of much money to be made, I felt like a flower wilting. The tap root of my life ultimately needing more depth, more water from the understory of my life. I longed to have my hands back in the soil. And so, with Beau's blessing, I jumped and left my day job, my 401K, my health insurance and all financial security.

Within a month's time, living in Topanga Canyon, I would meet a woman and a fellow earth steward. She hired me to put a crew together and build, with my own two hands, her beautiful garden, cutting down the eucalyptus trees in the front garden and chopping the wood. We would bring in stone from a local quarry and using physics and natural building techniques, we would corbel all the walls and build the patios, the planting beds and the herb spiral. We used the wood from the Eucalyptus to construct the arbors for grapes, an epic treehouse and the fences which we lined with thorny California native roses to keep the bunnies out. We would plant lots

and lots of oak-tolerant, drought-tolerant native plants that were all acquired locally. We would bring in soil and manure from the local equestrian center. We would plant the hillside with vegetables and herbs of all kinds, flowering and fruiting vines along the boundaries of the property.

I cared for this garden for several years. Three days a week I would tend the soil, water the plants, prune, plant, weed, and marvel at all the life flourishing in this garden where once there were just two trees. All the birds and wildlife and flowers and food, somehow in balance with each other. There was always enough for everyone and everything. I would harvest food for her and for Akasha, a restaurant in Culver City. Each week I would make fresh-cut bouquets for her family. It was a glorious experience and it paved the way for so much. I knew without a shadow of a doubt that I was doing exactly what I was meant to be doing. Gardening, even before I forged a deeper relationship with design, was soulful.

Garden design meets many of my desires, allowing me to work outside some days, as well as inside at my drafting table on others. I engage all of myself, which is such a blessing — my body, my mind and my creativity. Working in gardens creates conditions for me to collaborate with lots of interesting people, in diverse settings, assisting people in a way that feels functional and soulful. It allows me to make and reveal beauty while doing something good for the planet. No matter how many years of experience I build upon and the tributaries I follow, the heart and breath of what I do and why I do it has never changed. My intention has always been to work with plants and to help foster a relationship between myself and the natural world, between other people and the natural world. To help create a bridge of understanding between Mother Nature and Human Nature. Spending time in a garden, growing a garden, is a practice that not only fosters a deeper connection with Mother Nature, but our own nature and the nature of others. Leonardo Da Vinci said that water is the driving force of all of nature. Tuning in so we can source deep nourishment in life is like finding a wellspring of water where you thought there was only desert.

Like any great romance, there's love, there's compatibility and there's growth.

There is always more to learn. Twenty years in and this work continues to inspire and challenge me. I am always learning new skills, encountering new plants, meeting new people, experiencing new challenges in new spaces. Discovering new design ideas for inspiration, new building techniques, new cultures, new aspects of myself. There is always a growing edge, a balance between study and mastery. Choosing the path with heart creates conditions for all sorts of opportunities, revealing new paths, opening doors, expanding horizons and allowing us to live in time with the world we create, day by day.

I believe we all have a "nature," a way of being in the world, a certain pulse that we are attuned to. There's no point in trying to be who we are not. As we begin to trust in who we are and how we uniquely move through the world, we create flow.

Like water, we can learn to allow and trust the flow of life and at that, to allow and trust the story our life is telling through us. Like a river winding down a mountain and through a valley, we, too, can lean in to each twist and turn in our lives. To source water and keep growing in our lives, we sequester the lessons, harvest the nourishment and engage opportunities with those whom we share an affinity. Captained by our internal compass we come to know self trust. This self trust is necessary in order to allow ourselves to follow the tributaries of our passions, our inspiration and personal bliss so we can deepen our roots and expand our reach in the world. Learning to deepen our source of nourishment and follow the flow of life sometimes means we must surrender. Surrendering means leaning in and letting go, not resisting what is. This is freedom. This is how we allow life to work for us. There are no wrong turns. Each choice is a choice with endless opportunity to align, evolve and grow. Working with the flow of our life, trusting our nature and inner guidance systems, we cultivate trust and allowance in the world which we live in. Each moment creates the conditions for the next. Anchored within a sense of self, the various stories, chapters and transitions become integrated in uniquely supportive ways.

We get what we need when we need it. We all have places within the landscapes of our lives that we discover, often through twisted paths and challenges, to be wellsprings of strength, power and healing. Each bent branch, each twisted river finds its place and creates beauty. As we create space within to allow life to unfold, to allow wildness to be, we equally allow ourselves to drink in deeply the nourishment and the lessons of all of our experiences. We allow ourselves to be nurtured and strengthened by our experiences, good and bad, and we evolve.

All things are possible through design.

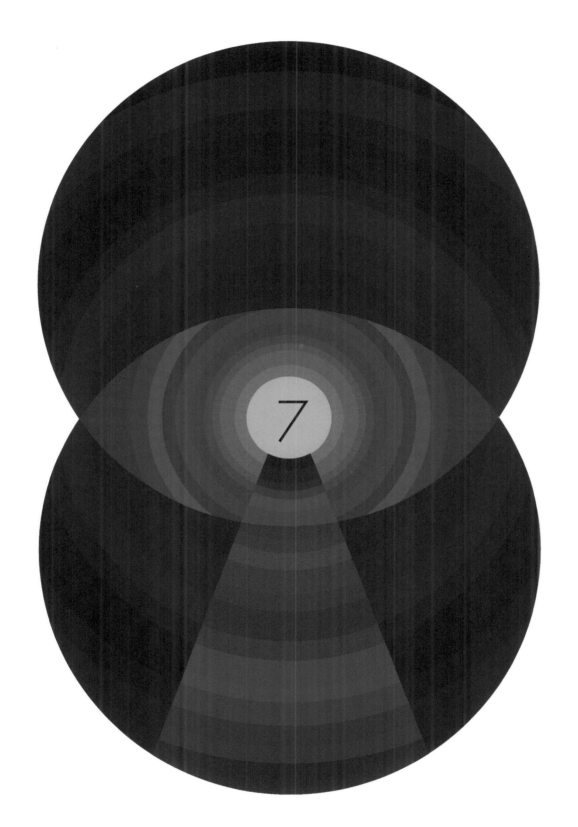

Backup Systems:
Multiple Elements
within a Single Function

NATURE ALWAYS HAS A BACKUP SYSTEM. It never puts itself in a corner, leaving itself only one means of survival. It constantly seeks ways of establishing relationships to ensure survival, sustainability and growth.

One of my favorite plants, Baccharis Pilularis, is an integral plant in the California landscape that prevents erosion on many hillsides. It emits a pheromone that attracts a select species of bird that has a specific function in ecological preservation and erosion. These birds come, they poop and nourish the soil around the plant, deepening and encouraging root growth. The plant grows root systems that are three times the size of the upper body, assisting further in preventing erosion along dry hillsides. This plant can tolerate extreme, dry heat and heavy, wet rains. It is oak-tolerant and evergreen. It features many elements that work towards a single function: keeping the hillside intact.

But Nature has a backup system, even for this magical plant. And as designers, we should keep backup systems in mind, too. If we are seeking to prevent erosion on a hillside, we want plants that attract beneficial insects and pollinators, won't compete with the indigenous habitat and relate harmoniously so that the root systems of various species can grow robust, together. We want to direct water through the use of berms and swales, optimizing water flow so that water is appropriately sequestered and integrated to irrigate the appropriate plants without drenching the hillside. We always seek to reinforce our intention with as many elements as possible.

This same Permaculture principle applies to how we design our lives. Ask yourself: Does your life design include backup systems of support? How does where you live, what you do to support yourself, how you relate to your family, how you relate to yourself, your personal practice, your art, how much money you make, your free time, all function in relationship to each other? Are there multiple elements reinforcing a single function — and does each element in your life support multiple functions? Are the various aspects of your life in support of one another or are they somehow creating conflict?

In one way, this principle speaks to the power of diversity. A healthy forest is alive and abundant because diverse elements contribute to its livelihood. There are plants of different ages and phases, some decomposing, some flourishing, some just sprouting; there are flowers and elemental components that create conditions for beneficial insects to keep the forest free from disease, for seeds and fruits to create conditions for birds and other animals that contribute to pollination and help build healthy soil.

However, the wisdom of a natural design understands that it is not simply diversity that creates balance in a system, but functional relationships between diverse elements that do. Sometimes distilling our lives down to the essential elements can help us see the common ground between those different elements, and understand how each component might be able to better support the others.

When I was 21 years old, I moved from Ithaca to San Francisco because it seemed like a vibrant, open-minded city immersed in nature, surrounded by mountains and oceans. I sold my car to buy a Ford Econoline Van to drive West. I had hair down to the bottom of my back— long, thick, curly black hair — and I cut it super short and sexy and set my neck free. I packed about a hundred pounds of rocks I had been collecting, all my books, some clothes and a couple of pairs of shoes. I said goodbye to my family and all my friends, and with tears in my eyes, hit the open road. I had never traveled much outside of New York and I had never been to California. My mind was blown with each westward mile. The sky, the mountains, the rivers, the landscape — growing deeper, more expansive, more vibrant as I made my way west toward the setting sun.

I spent a few weeks in the Four Corners area of the United States, exploring Chaco Canyon and Canyon de Chelley, spending time camping with the Navajo in Arizona, visiting the Hopi Reservation in New Mexico. A twenty-mile dirt road led into Chaco Canyon, where I met J.B. Cornucopia, an older white man with a long, white beard who was a ranger at the National Monument. He gave a lecture on astronomy and architecture in Chaco Canyon one evening, and I remember he said — while about 20 of us stared up at the big night sky — "We dance around the ring and suppose, while the secret stands in the center and knows."

These ancient "ruins" in the open expanses of desert or inside of cliffs had been built by hand by the ancient Pueblo/ Anasazi, thousands of years ago, and were designed with no separation between human nature and nature-nature. The future, past and present held in perfect balance through the architecture, which dictated a way of life that took in all aspects of living culture while allowing ecological functions to occur. J.B. Cornucopia's reflection on Chaco Canyon, and the incredible history its architecture emulates thousands of years later, speaks to how powerfully various elements relate to one another to contribute to an enduring culture or life. His words embody in poetry the strength of an orchestrated design wherein people build kivas or markets, skyscrapers or subways, and either way, there are multiple avenues of support which contribute to the success and stability of each function of life in the culture.

We live in a dynamic world. A good design fosters relationships with all components. The architecture is woven into the fabric of the culture and the culture reflects patterns of exchange, commerce, celebration, worship, agriculture and family. No one element exists on its own, nor does it exist in a freeze frame. Each element exists in endless moments in space and cycles in time.

In Permaculture, we often talk about needs, resources, and skills. When it comes to economic exchanges of energy, "free" is never sustainable. Instead, we create inventory lists of all of our needs, resources, and skills. A need is something you don't already have but is required to be healthy, happy, and safe. Money is not a need, but rather a means to meet a need — like a need for a home, food, job, ride, tool, or help with childcare. A resource is something you already own or have access to, like a garage, garden, car, computer or power tools. A skill is something you know how to do that can help others, like drafting, building websites, repairing cars, sewing, singing or operating a chainsaw. Money is just a vehicle for trading resources and skills to accommodate needs. We can compare and match our lists of needs, resources, and skills with those of others to discover new ways to support each other. We can begin to build backup systems within our relationships at large, our communities and our personal lives. We can do as nature does.

Some tangible examples of this principle at play include time banks, co-ops, and local currencies — viable, sustainable means of exchange that have worked for thousands of years. The goal is to diversify our skills and resources with a set intention, identify needs and common throughlines between various aspects of our lives, and then stack functions with other people in as many ways as possible, to maximize yield. But for these backup systems to work, there must be trust within the community and commitment to the whole. Relationships are at the heart of any sustainable system and design. Our relationships outward reflect the relationship inward.

Inspired by the soulful architecture of Chaco Canyon — and committed to building a support system for myself that I could expand upon and also attuned to the call in my own soul to find my link with the big sky and natural rhythms of my own life — I would eventually arrive in San Francisco. Chaco inspired me deeply. It revealed to me how to think of backup systems in an artful and integrated way. I understood that lifestyle in harmony with the planet and in community with others who feel the same is possible. My internal guidance led the way with a knowing that to discover my true path, a connection to the natural world was imperative. San Francisco is a fabulous city, but after growing up in New York, I didn't want to live in another city, miles from my family and everyone I loved. At least not yet and not at this time. Instead, I chose Fairfax, a little town north of San Francisco. A place that was nestled in the mountains, close enough to the city and the vibrant culture of city living, but connected by a strong community and an even stronger reverence to the natural world. It was here I would discover my deep love of plants, mostly by chance. It was here I would make friends for life, begin my study of Permaculture, gardening and ecology. Once again, a little twist and turn would find me squarely on the path, leading me to the truth of my soul's calling.

Any good design starts by identifying problems so we can discover solutions. Bill Mollison was an Australian author, researcher, scientist, teacher and biologist. He is one of the primary individuals in modern culture responsible for organizing and promoting the theory and practice of Permaculture. He once said there are an infinite number of solutions to any problem. The problems in a given landscape don't define the design but instead, guide the design towards the most efficient, and oftentimes creative, solution. By thinking outside the frame and considering all aspects of who we are and what we have to offer — our needs, resources, and skills — we can begin to discover viable, sustainable systems. We may not always know what stands in the center, but we can choose a point of reference, set an intention and then design backup systems to support our goals by forging relationships in more than one way. These relationships are internal and exist between aspects of who we are, what we love and need. And they exist in relationship to others, as we find ways of creating exchanges of support. Together we will always be stronger.

Invisible Work

by Alison Luterman

Because no one could ever praise me enough, because I don't mean these poems only

but the unseen

unbelievable effort it takes to live

the life that goes on between them,

I think all the time about invisible work.

About the young mother on Welfare I interviewed years ago,

who said, "It's hard.

You bring him to the park,

run rings around yourself keeping him safe, cut hot dogs into bite-sized pieces for dinner, and there's no one

to say what a good job you're doing,

how you were patient and loving

for the thousandth time even though you had a headache."

And I, who am used to feeling sorry for myself

because I am lonely,

when all the while,

as the Chippewa poem says, I am being carried

by great winds across the sky,

thought of the invisible work that stitches up the world day and night,

the slow, unglamorous work of healing,

the way worms in the garden

tunnel ceaselessly so the earth can breathe

and bees ransack this world into being,

while owls and poets stalk shadows,

our loneliest labors under the moon.

There are mothers

for everything, and the sea

is a mother too,

whispering and whispering to us long after we have stopped listening. I stopped and let myself lean

a moment, against the blue

shoulder of the air. The work

of my heart

is the work of the world's heart. There is no other art.

8

Recycling The Flow of Energy

YOU CAN TELL A LOT ABOUT THE HEALTH OF A SYSTEM BY LOOKING AT ITS WASTE. The natural world is always seeking to close loops, recycling byproducts as many times as possible. We are accustomed to living in a world of constant supply and we forget that the world, our lives and our relationships are governed by a system of inputs and outputs. Learning how to balance these inputs and outputs by recycling energy, to maximize yield with the least amount of effort, is key to any healthy relationship. Once again, we live within moments in space and cycles in time. Energy passes through our natural systems in a variety of ways, resulting in weather, water, trees, wind, fruits, plants, compost and so on. Energy is sequestered, harvested, consumed and recycled.

We build internal infrastructures with elaborate canals. We sequester love, we harvest affection, we consume generosity. Love, money, and relationships become a base form of accounting between people. It's hard to put into practice but the truth is we will never, ever, ever be able to experience the love, the money, the life and the fulfillment we want unless we embody it first, until we metabolize what we sequester and recycle back the beauty, the love, the generosity we have received. As we become a generous force of love, compassion or stewardship in the world, we create more of the conditions within ourselves to receive this from the world we live in.

Energy — money, love, lifestyle or personal happiness — is always coming from someplace and going some-place else. As we begin to map nature's whole-system models to our personal practices and lifestyles, we can consider how we sequester, harvest, consume and recycle energy. We can close feedback loops and allow each part of the process the space and time necessary to integrate and thus contribute whole-heartedly to the next phase.

These moments of love and loss can be big or small, but they are experienced by everyone in one way or another, in a human way. In a culture that can often seem heartless, it's easy to lose sight of the need to move through each stage of an experience fully. As a culture, we are not taught to honor death nor are we encouraged to grieve deeply when we experience loss. In this culture, we enamor life and happiness without considering its

counterparts with equal reverence and respect. It is through the process of grieving what we have loved and lost that we allow our lives the space to metabolize difficult experiences. In doing so, we learn the lesson of that experience and allow it to recycle back into our lives as wisdom, transforming us into more open-hearted, wholehearted people with a greater sense of depth, beauty and authentic relation to the world we live within.

As we deepen our relationship with ourselves and our emotional experiences, and as we come to understand that each place in the wheel is natural and necessary, we become containers for what we love, and as such, larger containers for whom we love. This in turn creates the conditions for deeper relationships with others, for connection and for reciprocity. We cannot have what we cannot give. If we can't embody it, we cannot resonate and receive it when someone comes along and tries to give it to us.

Life is constantly changing. We are constantly changing. Humans are co-evolving living systems.

It is through the soulful experience of honoring what we love and lose that we bring beauty back to our worlds, and discover what we love about being alive. We learn to recycle the fullness of each experience so we can create more beauty, so we can recycle the seasons of our lives, and consciously create the space for us to equally feel calm presence with ourselves, and ultimately compassion and self-love.

The more we allow ourselves to be real with the quiet, tender parts of ourselves that sometimes hurt to touch, the more capable we become of shining a light for ourselves in the darkness. Becoming to ourselves the ones we seek, discovering how to nourish ourselves in all seasons of living. By being real with what we grieve, or our vulnerabilities, our shame even, we allow ourselves to be transformed into more beautiful beings. We become humbled by life, tumbled like pebbles in water, made soft again as life rounds out our rough edges, offering us new and learned compassion. As we are tempered by the rain and the wind, we learn to be gracious, grateful and generous.

If you are unable to feel gratitude or practice simple recognition for what you are receiving on even a small level, you are moving from a place of lack. You are trapped by your own illusions of disempowerment and likely feel victimized by life, always needing more, consuming what you feel you lack and need like a vacuum — not engaged in your own life and creation as an active participant. If you cannot recognize what you are receiving, simple joys, simple gifts, and create the conditions in yourself to receive each wholeheartedly by practicing gratitude, you will not have energy to give, yourself or others, because it is not being sequestered in your spirit.

Giving of your energy, your time, your resources, your skills, is a practice with tremendous rewards that gives back tenfold. When we can offer ourselves in service to life, when we can sequester the lessons and the blessings and allow whatever it is that we are experiencing to usher in more beauty because of the heartbreak, we create the conditions within to give and then to receive back what it is we are offering.

This relationship is forever intertwined. For a relationship, with yourself or another, the capacity to give and receive must move freely in both directions. When it does, we can build communities and societies that share in the reciprocity of one another's wellness.

All of the great ancient indigenous civilizations understood this principle of recycling energy. They based their entire social structures on this concept.

In Peru, the Chakana Incan Cross/Andean Cross was then, and remains today, a symbol of sustainability. It was the guiding force in how the Inca designed Machu Picchu, along with many other settlements in their time.

Similar to the avocado "tax" or "tribute" asked by the Aztec kings in pre-Columbian civilizations, the Andean cross was a symbol for livelihood in Peru. The different aspects of the cross, moving down from top to the right, symbolize: the past (snake), the present (the puma) and the future (the condor). The knowing we come from one place and are going to another was embedded in the fabric of society. The Inca understood that in any moment they were connected to their past, their present and their future, and they paid respect to this in their daily lives.

The values upon which they built their civilizations, including Machu Picchu, were based on knowledge, community work, and obligatory work. Knowledge denoted a person of "wealth," as wealth was not tallied by material items but rather by the amount of overall knowledge a person possessed in terms of astronomy, law, natural sciences, agriculture, etc.

Community work was integral to society, because it was a society based on reciprocity. You would contribute in all ways possible to better the livelihood of your neighbor, knowing that, when your time of need came, your community would be there for you, as well.

Finally, there was obligatory work, meaning that your "tax" or "tribute" for being a part of society was to give of your skill, products and resources as only you could. The community would assess the intrinsic characteristics of each person and would ask them to give as they could. So, for example, if you were a musician, it was part of your offering to the community to sing or play music for the people who were building the structures for the community; or if you were a farmer you would contribute a percentage of your crop to the king, who would stockpile it for the entire community for times of need.

The three ethics, which governed all law and structures in both relationship and society in these ancient cultures, were: Wisdom, Work, and Reciprocity. Communities, like individuals, understood that we move through collective cycles in time, as all living systems on the planet do. When society encourages reciprocity within the culture, for give and take, recycling the flow of all energy throughout the process, we cultivate trust in each other. With trust, there is respect and tolerance for diversity. Within this respect for diversity are regenerative methods of support and new possibilities for creative expression. We are microcosms of the planet, both as individuals and as a society. We can emulate nature as a guide for a better world.

Nature is always recycling its flow and changing its form. It's not afraid to change. Clouds aren't afraid to roar and boom, creating thunder and lightning, and then become drops of water that rain to the ground and become part of the fabric of the soil, drunk by the plants, pulled back up to the tippy-tops of trees to change form yet again. Each place in the wheel, each moment in the cycle, has a purpose, a reason. The natural world doesn't reject itself or its processes the way we humans have been conditioned to do. In our pursuit of "happiness" or "success," it seems we often aspire to rise above the natural world we live in to find a perceived solace in a digitized or removed context. Perhaps we have been conditioned into inhabiting a space outside of natural rhythms and taught to believe an old story that nature, women, fear, the "other" is something to control, gain power over and force to submit. We disconnect from what is inherent and natural and then we wonder why we suffer such dis-ease.

Connecting to our own true nature no matter what is occurring in our lives and, to the true nature of another, even when they look different or don't share our point of view, is the supple softening needed to allow life to unfurl gracefully in a world of constant change. To let life happen and trust the process. We learn once again to sequester, harvest and recycle the lessons of living with as much beauty and honesty as we are willing to bring to it every day. Connecting to the natural world, to the subtle, the wild, the dark and the light, the seasons of time and the full totality of what it means to be living alive in a world that is constantly changing, is finding our place in the circle. We allow what breaks us to nourish and transform us so that we can lift up what we love most with greater power, greater beauty and greater awe.

9

The Edge Effect

PERMACULTURE DESIGN ALWAYS SEEKS TO REPLICATE NATURAL PATTERNS BY CREATING THE EDGE EFFECT WITH EDGE AND ECOTONES. In the landscape, an edge is the interface where two biological communities (for example, forest and valley) or two landscape elements (like land and water) come together. Ecotones occur where two ecological habitats meet, for example oak woodland and marine. The Edge effect in nature is the difference between a flat, non-porous surface with little edge or patten versus one that is permeable, has sharp contrasts in soil or hydrology, and is varying in pattern with lots of edge.

For example, concrete on a sidewalk in a suburb on a hill has very little edge. Concrete is not permeable and is often flat and homogeneous when used to make a sidewalk. When rain comes down onto an angled hill, the water flowing down the sidewalk has nowhere to go, and becomes sheet flow with the potential to cause destruction. At the very least, we have missed an opportunity to sequester and harvest the water, a valuable resource. As holistic designers we want to create an edge, assuming there is no reason not to. We want to find a way to moderate the flow of water, in this case down a hill, so that we can sequester and harvest it for use within the landscape. We might break up the concrete, increase gaps at joints between the slabs, remove the concrete and regrade the hill using berms and swales to catch water, or plant trees and gardens along the swales and berms to encourage the water to recycle itself back into the system.

When we create edge, we create the opportunity for things to happen. And we avoid unnecessary waste.

When the soil is receptive and filled with edge, a garden can grow. Water can permeate the soil. Diverse plants can take root and grow and create conditions for life to flourish. We create an edge in our personal lives when we challenge ourselves to imagine and act just beyond our own limitations — when we allow our ideas to become more porous. This is how we push ourselves to grow. We create edge on an interpersonal level when we create conditions for new patterns to emerge and new relationships to occur by stepping outside of our comfort zones, interacting with people who stimulate us because they are different from us. Art and innovation on the cutting edge of culture push the society to evolve. Without edge, we have a very limited palette. When we are able to personally, interpersonally and collectively create conditions for a diverse range of elements to interact, we can observe where there is affinity, what patterns emerge, and what sticks. We use the principles of Permaculture to problem solve and trust in the power of diversity.

Who you are in this moment is partly a reflection of your nature, the intrinsic qualities that make you who you are, and a summation of your experiences. Consider then the infinite possibilities of your potential that you simply have not experienced yet. Interacting with new people who are outside of your normal safe-zone creates an edge, cultivates compassion, and fosters understanding. Compassion and understanding deepen relationships, and relationships are at the heart of all Permaculture systems. Going after that new job or new career, or developing a hobby that you have always wanted to pursue but felt you couldn't, creates an edge. Moving beyond fear and stretching your personal edge is an engaging and enlightening way to discover parts of yourself, your spirit and your heart that you never knew were there.

To arrive at my beloved profession, I needed to stretch my own edge. I didn't go to school to become a landscape designer. Or a gardener. Or a businesswoman. (Or a mother or a partner or a friend!). I got a B.F.A. in Acting from a conservatory in New York. Everything that has been worth anything in my life has existed outside of my initial comfort zone and has required courage, risk and willingness. With each personal stretch beyond my perceived edge, and the discomfort and ultimate transcendence of each rite of passage, I have discovered a vast sky of possibility within. The risks and challenges in my life have created strength, flexibility, and resilience. These qualities then cultivate further and deepen with time, like ridges of a mountain. Each expansion creates the condition for more expansion. And with that, more trust, within and without. I continually refine the art of being human through craft and practice. It's in the living of life that life comes alive.

In yoga we stretch and breathe to keep the shapes we create within our body alive, new each day. We learn to stay balanced in our breath so that we can stretch beyond ourselves, revolve around ourselves, from the gut, from the bones. We breathe with where we are, new each day, so that we have a chance to expand beyond ourselves and reach the goal: to experience union with self. Union with our nature.

As we do in our gardens, understanding what it means to live on the growing edge of life, to create an edge in our lives, is to live with trust in the way things work, step by step, moment by moment, day by day. It's trusting that when you jump, you are not going to fall. It may not be comfortable. Sometimes we even bear some bruises and scars, but those scars can help, and will heal you and others. When we allow our broken edges, our vulnerable parts, our perceived holes or messy, irregular and bloody hearts to be, as they are, we create an opportunity for something to happen. When we create space for opportunity, we can experience life on a new level, with soft, renewed skin. Open and receptive to the winds of time. We create an opportunity to be met in ways beyond ourselves. We create an opportunity to reach, expand and assist another, to be of service in the world. When we allow the growing edge to push us up and out, we create an opportunity for water to reach our roots, down and in. We can then be nourished by life systems bigger than we are — and to grow through cracks in the sidewalk.

The Edge illuminates the path forward. Groups outside of the dominant culture give us insight into how we are evolving as a culture at large. We are inspired by "cutting edge" artists or designers, thinkers and movement makers. Our world and opportunities expand and evolve because of what one person, somewhere, believed to be possible and took steps to make happen. From electricity to airplanes, vaccines to smartphones, we are constantly expanding and changing, shifting and evolving. We must consider the whole picture and all the moving parts so that we can evolve in an integrated way on a dynamic and changing planet. No one part is disconnected from the others. One part of the knot moves and indeed the whole knot shifts.

The goal is not to design our lives to avoid experiencing the ups and downs of being alive. But, rather, to embrace natural aliveness and design our lives with edge, to give ourselves the opportunity to evolve, to live the solutions and the lessons. To live a life worth living.

Any significant, valuable relationship, from our professional to our personal lives, requires and encourages growth and pushes us beyond our edge. Sometimes we just need to get out of the way and let our life tell the story it was meant to tell, through us. Sometimes we need to let go just enough to allow for free play, to allow ourselves to come to know deeply what it means to really trust the heart of our experiences — and live boldly from that place. How can we trust another if we cannot trust ourselves, trust that we are held in the heart of life and, more importantly, within our own hearts? How can we expect to trust another and cultivate sustainable relationships within families or communities if we cannot cultivate self-trust?

I was just a few months into a new relationship, on the brink of a collapsing economy that halted construction and landscaping, when I found out I was pregnant. I did not have the option to freak out, the luxury to lose my shit. I had to move immediately towards a solution. I refused to abandon my vision, not out of stubbornness, but because my life has always listened to this song of the sea, the language of plants. Instead of landscaping gardens, I would landscape the human body. I began making beautiful, asymmetrical necklaces with gold-plated crystals, amulets and gems that I had collected on trips to Peru and Mexico, interesting chains and combinations of fabric which hung in unique ways to accentuate the curves and natural movement of a body in space

and in time. Intent on forging a connection between plants and gardens and people, I transferred knowledge from the garden to frame the body. I engaged people to care for plants as part adornment, part power piece, part humility. These pieces, which hung down a person's back and equally down the front in unique ways, not always the same from one side to the other, but always balanced, enticed a person to feel their body, want to nourish the plant, engage with others, foster a connection. I wanted to create a relationship between Mother Nature and Human Nature, the body and the bone, the rock and the respite. So I integrated tiny, custom-cast, gold-plated branches that held air plants, which you could attach to the necklace as a way of acknowledging that your life, your body, was a garden. Of drawing awareness to the ways in which a stone feels draped down the nape of our neck or along the back, or around our breasts.

This little venture, a life on the edge for a single, pregnant woman, was inspired and honest. I gained some press and was able to launch a business, Viola Living Jewels.

Nonetheless, I needed a home with nominal rent. I needed a place where I could rest at ease in my body so my child could learn that from me. I needed a place to grow. I made up my mind years ago to not waste my precious energy worrying about money. Of all the things to worry about, worrying about money was the most boring and futile. Instead, I made a commitment to show up even more fully, more presently, more creatively in my life.

As life would have it, my dear friends offered me a trade (aha, matching needs to resources and skills!): I would help them with some domestic work and organization while they were out of the country and anticipating their first child — and in return, they would offer me their oceanfront home in Venice Beach. I was so financially

strapped and so humbled by the changes unfolding and yet here I was, safe, supported by my community and supporting this child inside. Every day I would go down to the ocean and sing to this baby growing in my belly. I would sing to make sense of a future that was beyond my awareness, that my head could not quite wrap itself around, but a future that I knew I was at the heart and helm of.

Vianna was born a few days past the Fall Equinox, a time of the year when there is perfect balance between day and night, on the advent of a new season. Everything about her blessed life, from conception to birth, was sacred and filled my life with the winds of change. When I left the beach, I ended up back on the eastside of LA, focused on developing a solid, sustainable career doing what I loved to support me and this child.

And I did it. Hands in the dirt and head below the heart, one step at a time, over thousands of hours, I regenerated my design business and committed myself to my purpose and passion with more zest, more focus, more intention.

Which is not to say life is a fairytale. There have been many difficult and trying days and moments, but with practice, I have learned to trust my ability to stay balanced and focused as life around me changes, as I change, as I encourage myself to grow beyond myself, always, with the intention to keep my heart and head aligned. Always seeking and embracing the edge.

Where there is edge there is possibility, there is expansion and growth. When we can extend ourselves beyond, we evolve.

"Ring the bell that still can ring, forget your perfect offering.
There is a crack in everything. That's how the light gets in."

-Leonard Cohen

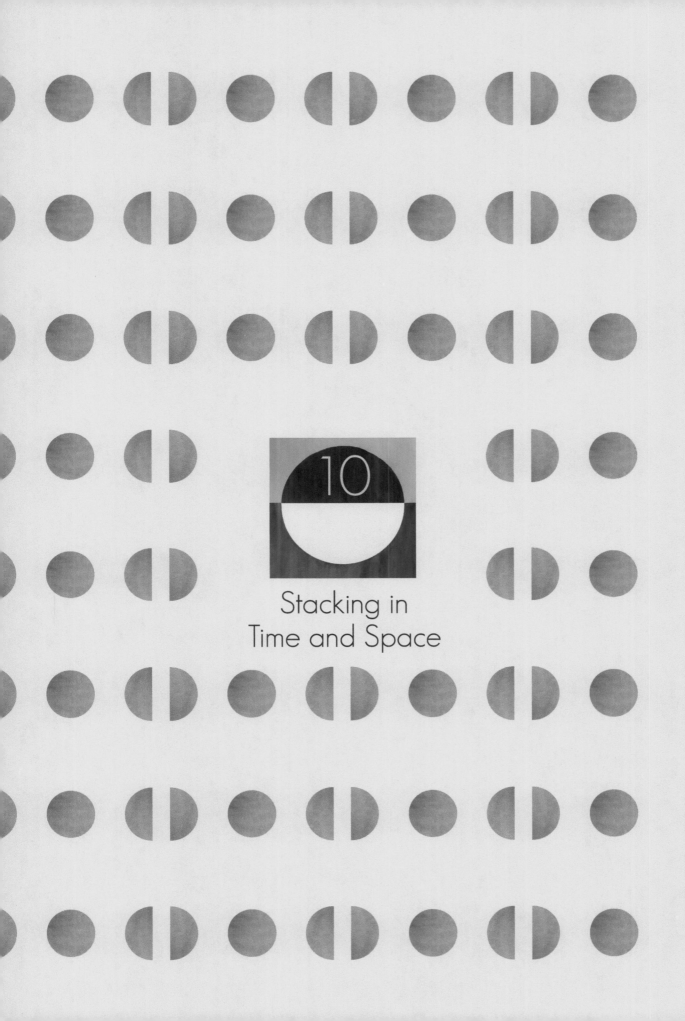

10

Stacking in
Time and Space

THE WORLD HAS NEVER BEEN A PLACE. It has always been a process.

We live in a world that is constantly changing. We, right now, are experiencing a moment in space and a point in a cycle in time. We are coming from one place and moving towards another in a series of moments, stacked in time. We look to find ways to stack efforts and energy such that everything does multiple things at once. In this way, we maximize yield, producing abundance with the least amount of energy. To keep the system in balance, we seek functional connections between inputs and outputs.

Stacking is a Permaculture design technique that finds this connection and combines several efforts with similar intentions to satisfy multiple ends in time and space.

For example, we stack several appointments for one trip across town instead of driving back and forth for each one separately. Or, we might plant California Wild Rose in a garden on the west coast. California Wild Rose makes a beautiful tea high in Vitamin C with medicinal rose hips, it attracts many different types of pollinators, and creates a thicket that is habitat for birds and a barrier for critters. Functions stack. Another example: compost piles that break down food scraps and organic waste and then convert them into fertile amendments for soil. If we add chickens to the mix, they turn the pile, which is imperative, and their droppings create nitrogen, which helps break down masses of carbon, like leaf piles. The chickens eat anything and everything in the pile, deterring any critters or insects that might be a nuisance. Further, the pile creates a food source for the flock and a no-work-required solution for chicken poop. Many functions stack to create a balance between inputs and outputs.

We can just as easily apply this principle to the invisible structures of our lives. Consider where common ground exists amongst various aspects of your life, and how you might be able to stack efforts to streamline outcomes and satisfy multiple ends in different parts of your life. When we learn to identify the components that make up our lives, both in space and in time, we receive an opportunity to discover connections and relationships between aspects of our life that may seem polarized. Through the practice of stacking our energy, resources and time, we might find that we can satisfy several needs or goals with one action. In doing so, we discover a renewed sense of holistic perspective.

In order to discover new ways of stacking functions, we need to be willing, once again, to think outside of the box and rearrange how we organize our lives at large. We need to maintain a birds-eye view long enough to see clearly the inputs and outputs that make up our lives, to see the varying elements that comprise its substance, and to consider how the elements and aspects of our lives, in time and space, relate to each other. We need to be willing to turn the frame upside down and inside out — and see things from a new perspective without fear. Nothing of great importance or significance can be designed from a place of fear. Fear cuts off the creative impulse before it begins. I have found that it is often the fear of change, not the change itself, that creates obstacles. Which is not to say we instigate fear to prove a point or wear blinders. Rather, we learn to consider the whole picture and respond thoughtfully rather than react impulsively, and so we can choose our actions wisely.

We make choices. Then, as we learn and experience and move through the world, or a space, or a garden, we often make new and better choices along the way. Our lives, our gardens, our spaces change in time. As we come to understand how all the components work together, we can continue to refine the relationships between the various elements to make the components more effective and harmonious. Self-trust teaches us that we don't need to worry so much about the details of the future. As long as we maintain an open and present relationship with ourselves and our lives, we will be there for ourselves down the line, able to solve any problems that arise.

As a designer, I constantly remind myself that nothing is set in stone. Creativity breeds more creativity. Creativity flourishes when we remember to not get stuck in perceiving our lives, and our gardens, in just one way, but to seek the perspective needed to see how all the parts move together. To remember that there are often new shapes or ways of moving through a space that we may not have considered yet. We can arrange a space and then rearrange it as our needs change, as we grow into the person we are becoming.

For six years I lived in one house in Highland Park, a suburb just outside of downtown LA. When I moved in, 6 months pregnant, there were two dry and flat lawns, one in front and one in back. No plants, no garden beds, no earthworms. Nothing. Just the lawn and some cinder block walls. I could always see the potential. I broke clay soil and planted butterfly bushes in patches of earth that had long since been abandoned. Over time, following the birth of my daughter Vianna, I would build my business to support us both, design and plant a garden with a baby strapped to my chest, get married, get divorced, plant many more gardens, and turn those two lawns into thriving garden spaces with flowers of all colors, a host of birds and butterflies, hummingbirds of different colors, food, herbs, shade trees. That single house held space for some of the greatest and hardest times of my life. That single house lived many lives.

I rearranged furniture with each transition. I painted walls. I took cuttings. I sourced plugs of geranium and lavender as tiny as my pinky, I saved all the broken, unwanted and discarded plants I could find. I recycled old pebbles and concrete pavers and, little by little, I transformed the space into a living, moving, delightful garden, sown with a heartbreaking joy. Wild, experimental, evidence of all the various choices I had made, and then remade, over the years.

In that one house I ran a business, became a mother, and a real, tumbled woman. I fell in and out of love in that house. I cooked for my daughter and friends nearly every night. I had people come through while others worked in the studio or in the garden, Vianna jumping on a pogo stick or climbing her dome or swinging from her yoga trapeze. I partitioned the house to satisfy work needs and make space for V to play. I hosted classes for her preschool and invited the kids over to harvest pumpkins and watermelons, observe caterpillars and cocoons, throw wildflower seeds, create art with little pieces of flowers and plants and glue, and I enjoyed watching Vianna spearhead these little creations. I learned to run a business and juggle being a single mother in a house that was very alive in all respects. There was only so much space, and I had to keep things flowing with work to maintain primary support for V and me, and to keep the river flowing in a stable current for my crew and employees. Looking back, there wasn't a whole lot of space for me in the house, but I figured out how to live surrounded always by others.

As business grew and the summers took hold, the layers of time would tell many stories in that house, some wonderful and some very sad, and the garden always held it all. There were many moments I spent with my head in my hands and bare feet in the soil, praying for peace, planting seeds, learning to meditate deeper, learning to sit with all that was happening, with the magnificent unfolding and with the deep unearthing of old pains. Learning to sit with the realization that my heart had grown and that new love was taking root.

I taught myself new drafting techniques and practiced as often as I could on each new project. My time working in the studio (aka my garage) was cut short by some obstacles: An infestation of black widows and pantry moths; bigger jobs that required more concentration, computers and people who needed AC to stay cool in summer; and finally, a leaking roof in winter. Vianna was also growing older, out of diapers and contained spaces, spiraling out in her natural succession of childhood and needing more space to run and jump and move through her world. Everything was growing bigger. Birthday parties, outdoor dinners, drafting tables in the garage and eventually in the living room, stored materials of gravel or plants and leftover stones taking over the space for various jobs. Another infestation, this time … rats. My life was stacked with multiple inputs and outputs, but life evolved, time moved on. I grew, V grew, my business grew — my life evolved and the balance tilted off center.

I sensed it was time to move on. But how to find a space I could afford for my business that would be accessible to clients in north Malibu and throughout the city proper and offer space for tools, plants, a drafting studio and office, as well as a sanctuary for my private life? I began to wonder how I could keep Vianna's deep curiosity for the natural world alive, a curiosity she had cultivated in the garden with me, while delivering her to the next chapter in life, and helping to find a great school in which she could flourish. I envisioned a new space for Vianna to experience childhood close to nature, to make art, study science, and grow in a good community with a great school. And of course, for myself, a place I could thrive creatively, spiritually, and emotionally. Once again, I understood the puzzle but could not see yet how all the pieces were to come together. How the functions would stack in time and space. It all had to change, though I wasn't sure how. I packed boxes even though I didn't know where we were going. I condensed my office, started to prune and weed and make space for what could come next.

One June afternoon, I was driving through Topanga Canyon. As I took the bend up Old Canyon, it occurred to me that I was actually looking for Topanga everywhere else in LA. And when I came there, I was trying to convince myself to not move back. It was such a curious revelation, and I asked myself why. The answer was obvious. In my efforts to usher my business and my baby through their early years, I had stopped thinking of myself, of considering my own needs. I was thinking of everyone around me — ex-husbands, my boyfriend, friends, and employees. In a completely quiet, simple, pure moment, I said aloud: "I'm moving back here. I don't know how or when, but I will stay open. I want an open, clean and fresh space in which my business, V and I can thrive." I called the school, wondering if there was a waitlist or if enrollment would be a struggle. "If you live here, you just come in and enroll. She can start the next day." "That's it?" I asked. "That's it."

Driving downtown 20 minutes later, I told a friend I wanted to move back to Topanga. She is a realtor and sent me a few listings. I casually opened the link that night and the first thing I saw was a greenhouse and the road sign: "Happy Trail." That was it. I knew. We contacted the landowner, set up an appointment and, like a miracle, within days, the lease was signed, deposit down. V graduated preschool and we moved. I had a fabulous school for Vianna, an acre of land next to a creek, space for all my tools and belongings, a gorgeous new studio space, and was closer to many of my clients. Open, clean and fresh. Stacked perfectly in space and in time, with room to grow.

I know now that I will never have it all fully figured out from the start — not in business, not in a project, not in love, not in life — but I trust my ability to make the best decisions at every step of the way and to look back and then ahead. I am finally learning to believe that I have the stamina and strength to show up for whatever life deals me. It doesn't only matter how we feel or think, it matters most what we do. Things do fall into place. We need to get out of the way and rise to meet our lives and then let things unfold. Align our thoughts with our purpose and passion, prioritize what matters most, conceptualize a vision for how they can work together and take the next right step.

Creating with nature and following the signs of natural succession allows for the possibility to discover parts of ourselves we didn't know existed and to stack effort, purpose and function in all kinds of new, creative ways.

As a designer, I start with an overall map and keep my finger on the pulse of what inspires my action, what the overall goal is, and then allow for space to create while staying focused. I dream of the possibilities beyond the demolition and I try to encourage my clients to dream, too. As a Permaculture designer, I move from patterns to details, from dreams to reality, and I have learned to trust my ability to strategize and figure out what I need to, when I need to.

Stacking in time and space is to be in touch with what is at the heart of our endeavors and find ways to satisfy multiple needs and purposes with one action. Step by step, note by note, seed by seed, we create a symphony for living joyously.

Stay open to an unknown future, trusting that things will work out and that if you are living authentically, and taking honest stock of your evolving needs, new paths forward will present themselves to you, new paths that allow you to stack your needs in time and space.

"*How wild it was to let it be.*"

\- Cheryl Strayed

11

Biological Resources

AS PERMACULTURE DESIGNERS, WE ALWAYS SEEK BIOLOGICAL SOLUTIONS BEFORE TECHNOLOGICAL SOLUTIONS. Bill Mollison said, "The problems of the world grow increasingly complex, while the solutions remain embarrassingly simple. We are too often too quick to jump to easy fixes, technological rescues, or other means of allopathically treating symptoms, without thinking of what created the problem in the first place." It is our job, our calling, to focus first on identifying what has caused the problem we hope to solve.

In the garden, the go-to for many is to treat issues with a fertilizer or chemical or technological Band-Aid, without addressing why something is happening. Many try to treat the symptom, which often causes further harm and disease to plants, insects (like bees) and soil, not to mention humans, birds, fish and animals. If indicators of disease or imbalance appear in a garden — for example, leaves start turning yellow, a plant suffers from a fungus, there is an abundance of a certain weed on a hillside that needs erosion control, there is an influx of gophers or moles, or an infestation of aphids, and on and on down the horizon line — we want to first ask what is creating the conditions for the problem. This is our point of departure to understand why things are happening. Is there a mineral deficiency in the soil? What is the relative location of certain plants to, let's say, the oak tree, or the sun? Is there too much or too little water? Has the earth been overgrazed? Has someone planted ivy or ice plants, which do nothing to encourage a holistic retention of hillside soil and, once removed, leave the soil barren and receptive to "weeds"? What is creating the condition for aphids, or gophers? What eats aphids or gophers?

As Permaculture designers, we consider how we might create different conditions while still employing solutions that benefit the whole.

To employ biological resources and solutions, we must be thoughtful and committed. Biological solutions are integrated with the natural world, with whole systems, and with people. They don't work against any part of the whole — or for the benefit of just one. We habitually try to convert ecosystems to the human experience rather than allowing ecological functions to occur, and adapting our human behaviors accordingly. As we learn to study a system — our body, our mind, our garden, our community — we can use the principles of Permaculture as a roadmap towards better understanding the biological resources of that system. As we come to understand the patterns at play, and how they inform the detailed functions within the system, we can begin to advocate for and integrate more intelligent and benevolent antidotes to problems we face in our gardens and in our hearts.

Permaculture design is not simply a selection of techniques, technologies, and tools. It's the toolbox itself. In it are all the tools, techniques, and technologies, with all the cultural, intellectual and natural relevance you need.

To map this principle to your personal experience, consider where imbalances exist within you. Do you suffer from anxiety or depression? Are your relationships fulfilling and healthy? Is your body strong and vibrant? Are you comfortable in your body? Do you feel connected to your passion, your purpose, and your path? Do you feel connected to the people you love in your life? We are all living systems, so there is always room for evolution, room to change and grow and mature and learn and hopefully, over time, to become more awesome and actualized versions of ourselves.

We come from one place and move towards another. The way forward is up to us.

As kids, we were all programmed with conditions that have been learned and passed down through families and within cultures for generations. Over the course of a lifetime, crisis can repeatedly surface conditions that create pleasant or unpleasant experiences. Some people turn to religion to make sense of their habituations, believing the answer is up and out there somewhere, with a god above that will shine a light and show the way. Others turn to science, the intellect, the mind, psychology, to uncover clues and piece together a narrative for overcoming difficulties in their lives. Still other traditions encourage us to dive within and discover, from a somatic place, the conditions inside the body and the soul, so that we might re-imagine those patterns and effect change. Whatever the course, the bottom line is that there are systemic impulses that create patterns which can culminate in joy and happiness — or create division and pain. In order to move beyond patterns of abuse or disconnect, not just for ourselves but for our children, we need to get to the root of the problem. We need to mix intellect and metaphor so that the body, mind and soul can heal.

For me, learning to tolerate the emotional impulse when triggered long enough to feel what I need so that I can then break the habitual response and make a new choice has been very powerful. Over the course of 5 years, I found out I was pregnant (with my daughter's father whom I had been dating for just a few months), experienced a major decline in work due to the economic recession, grew a baby in my belly while living in my friends apartment in Venice, found a home with Vianna's father, had a baby for the first time and became a mother, got married, rebuilt and expanded my business to support myself and our child, got divorced one year later, and then endured a nearly two-year custody battle. Within that year of marriage, all my glass houses shattered. I became a broken version of myself. I didn't yet know about gaslighting or narcissist personality disorder. I was so enmeshed in codependency that I needed to relive the pain of my own attachments in order to break free and chart a new path. During this time, I was maligned and slandered by people I once loved and trusted, endured the throes of a very difficult custodial war, lost every penny I had ever saved, went into debt, and learned through it all how to not fight or run, but to evolve.

Suffice to say, my inner landscape was rocked to the core and had to be completely realigned. Six weeks before our wedding, my daughter's father was struggling and had a breakdown. He started seeing a psychologist and I joined him to be supportive. His relationship with him was short lived, but I stayed on for years and to this day. Very few people close to me knew how much I was suffering during this time, all the while planning a wedding. Trying to keep our daughter safe and provide a solid base — emotionally, spiritually, mentally and financially — for her while my soon-to-be ex was unraveling was leading to my own spiritual demise. The worse things got, the more I isolated myself. I was scared to tell anyone close to me what was really going on, thinking they would judge him (and us). I became increasingly distraught and dissociative. The truth is, healing could not really take hold until I was pushed by circumstance to look deeply within myself to understand why I was tolerating the gaslighting, the verbal abuse, the manipulation, the lies, the humiliation. Ten years earlier I would have judged myself for ending up in that experience. Yet that relationship, in large part because of my love for our daughter, very humbly taught me a lot — not just about the patterns of relating that I inherited from my upbringing, and about my tolerance for abuse and codependency, but also about my resiliency, strength, wisdom and capacity for evolution. I learned what I was made of.

Marriage was not the solution for me. In fact, if I am honest, I knew from the moment I got pregnant with my daughter's dad that he and I were not compatible. But I was overly concerned with doing what I thought was "best" for our daughter, or trying to work out something that was impossible to work out on the level we both were at at that time. I was scared to disappoint family members or simply, fail. I made the mistake of not listening to myself when my soul, my intuition, my body spoke to me. I would learn a hard lesson and, in the end, I had no one to blame but myself. Discomfort, distress and dis-ease happen by NOT listening and choosing to act out of fear.

The moment I found the courage to be honest and real about what I knew needed to happen, what I needed to do, and where I needed to put my energy so that I could address the change within myself, as difficult as the initial shift was, my entire life — spiritual, physical, mental and emotional — transcended and improved. I had to look within and use the inherent biological resources of my being and my life to create a systemic change — strengthening my mindfulness practice, my physical yoga practice, doing the work I needed to in therapy to unravel the mental habits and imprinting, restructuring the material layout of my lifestyle and financial inputs and outputs to create balance, flow and health. Through it all I learned to integrate the living practice of Permaculture from within.

These days, I have great respect and reverence for my intuition. I listen. I listen to my intuition. I listen to my body. I listen and pay attention to the indicators present. I listen to what is not being said as much as what is. I take the time to regularly check in with who I am and where I am. I trust my gut when it comes to decisions I need to make to benefit Vianna and how to follow the best path possible as her mother. I have stopped trying to build relationships where there is no water and instead, mind my business and allow myself to do the work I need to do within to allow myself to live the life I am meant to live. I know

what it feels like to be so scared and alone and anxious and distraught and I know what it feels like to move through those experiences and thrive not in spite of them but because of them. I know today that my life can help someone else heal. But only because I found a way to help myself heal.

If we consider our bodies and physical health, how often do we use medications that do not alter the conditions but simply mask the symptoms? What about our mental and spiritual health? How do we interact with our own discomfort — or the discomfort of other people? It takes courage to look within, at all the patterns we have been taught and have adopted, and to review how they are serving us. Do they bring us into greater natural peace, or away from natural peace? If we can learn to look to ourselves, our thoughts, our actions, before confusing our circumstance by outsourcing our "problems" onto others, we might find we have more resources available than we originally believed.

When we are balanced, life unfolds in grace.

We live on a planet with tremendous biological resources, remedies and intelligent methodologies that have worked for millennia. We can learn how to heal our bodies, our spirits and our emotions, as well as our community relationships, our economies and our gardens, naturally. We can use principles of natural design to arrive at

biological solutions before imposing chemicals or technologies. Natural and holistic solutions. Modern technologies have a place in the world, without a doubt, but as we improve and strengthen our foundations, our systems — personally, interpersonally, environmentally — also improve and begin to thrive.

Our bodies are amazingly intelligent. Our planet is amazingly intelligent. By learning how to decode the language that is already programmed in us, our own natural resources and abilities to heal and create, we can begin to use what we have available differently and more appropriately.

Many people still believe the answers they seek exist beyond themselves. They seek to feed the hungry Buddha within by chasing "more." The time I spent in the Amazon taught me a lot about biological resources built into the physical environment and our bodies. As gardeners, we know that to harmonize a situation, we sometimes must remove, not add, whatever is creating the imbalance. Letting go is an art.

When my daughter was five, she said: "Mom, it's OK to let go of the good things in life. That's how you make space for something better. And something better is coming for you. And for me. I promise." Wow. I take her words to heart and try to remind myself that when I get attached or worried or am resisting some part of my life that I don't like, that it's just my thoughts, it's just temporary, and it will pass. I practice mindfulness whenever possible to connect to my intuition, the space in between my thoughts, so that I am able to maintain increasingly better harmony within myself. World peace starts within.

To experience our bodies, our spirits, our thoughts, our relationships, in their natural states — in the fullness of their biological resources — is to touch the essence of what is divine in this world, outside of spiritual belief or ideology. Simply, we learn to allow ecological functions to occur. Removing toxins from our bodies allows our bodies to work. Removing distractions, emotional blocks, disruptive thoughts, and sometimes toxic people, allows us to experience more harmony within.

We have all that we need to create the life we dream of, to experience love, happiness, and abundance. We are given the opportunity to experience life in our bodies here on this planet with other people. Our bodies hold an incredible amount of energy and intelligence, and yet we continue to think there is some magic formula we need to uncover to understand what is going on. This is because we forget the language to decode the feedback loops. So we play the game of thinking "when this happens" or "if that happens," finally, "it will all be okay and then I will be happy."

We learn to dismiss ancient and holistic teachings as "new age" phenomena or spiritual hype. We seek binary understandings of the world, ones we can label and name and define, box in, and, somehow, control. When we siphon ourselves off from the ways in which we naturally move through the world and experience life, the natural ways in which the world moves with us, especially in difficult moments or trials, we cut ourselves off from the very life force that feeds and regenerates our being.

What if we are perfect as is? What if we have already been forgiven? What if our planet is perfect and it's our perception of it that needs healing?

Nature's remedies always grow alongside the poison. Soap root is the antidote to poison oak, and they grow right next to each other under the canopy of the oak. Species and ideas co-evolve to cultivate life. The oak and the blue jay have evolved over thousands of years to keep West Coast hillsides in place. In one year, a blue jay will disperse 30, 0000 acorns. It forgets where 10% are. That 10% becomes oak trees and creates the oak woodland habitat that is home to the second largest bird population in the world, second only to the Amazon. The problem is the solution. Lean Into It.

Which is to say that it takes a deep curiosity and stable internal presence to not dismiss every discomfort or "poison," but to first develop an awareness of where to find the remedy. This is why in Permaculture, we lean into problems as gateways to discovering solutions, both within and without.

Our planet has sustained itself through natural catastrophes and destruction over and over, repairing itself, repairing relationships, rebuilding, restructuring. We can, too. We have all of the biological resources we need already. There is a Buddhist saying that reminds us "a butterfly with a hole in its wing lands on my finger … we do not need to be perfect to fly."

CONSIDER HOW MANY PROBLEMS WE COULD ELIMINATE BY SIMPLY PUTTING THINGS TOGETHER DIFFERENTLY. Ecosystems grow and flourish not only because of the intrinsic characteristics of elements and conditions, but because of how those elements and conditions function in relationship to each other. How might a shift in perspective or placement of an object, or a feeling, change the whole relationship for the better?

We live in a dynamic, moving, breathing world that is incessantly and persistently alive, all the time — as are we. Einstein said: "Any intelligent fool can make things bigger and more complex. It takes a touch of genius — and a lot of courage — to move in the opposite direction." As we simplify our perceptions and use our creativity to survey different ways in which we can put things together, possibilities unfold. Turn an idea upside down, inside-out, and explore all arrangements. Especially the ones you are afraid to consider. We are each here to express our creative genius (or let our creative genie move through us!). With mindfulness, we learn to move through the world, recognizing and accepting the gift that change affords us. To maintain an open and flexible mind in a world structured to encourage just the opposite takes courage. But that is our natural way. Everything we need is already within our capacity and within the capacity of what we create. It sometimes just needs new expressions and the right placement.

There are natural systems of reciprocity and cooperation that increase by the power of relative location. Ecosystems flourish not just because of what they offer, but where they exist in relationship to each other.

Integrated holistic solutions are the groundwork for a sustainable whole-system, wherein everything is included and integrated instead of isolated and compartmentalized. Like the roots of the redwood trees, which are some of the shallowest roots for the tallest trees on the planet. These giants survive their great height and encourage new growth by, essentially, "holding hands" beneath the surface of the soil and growing in groves around their mother. The leaves fall to the ground, creating mulch and conditions for a host of plants and wildlife that benefit the overall conditions. Eventually, when the mother-tree dies,

she falls to the ground and changes form again, becoming mulch that hosts moss, mycelium, maybe a beaver, birds, and epiphytes, eventually becoming part of the soil again. In the rich compost of her remains are born her offspring. And the cycle continues.

I've always marveled at the people who we stay close to in life for many years, where the relationship becomes a wellspring of support in and of itself, regenerating health and wellbeing for all. We all have different needs for space and closeness. We learn ways of attaching in relationships and building friendships. The right amount of space and the relative location of the relationships we treasure weaves the web of life around us, which can create joy, ease, inspiration — or pain.

Our intuition is not emotion. And emotions are different from feelings. Emotions are reactions in your body to the thoughts in your head. Emotions are also reactions in your mind to the feelings in your heart. So emotions can overwhelm feelings in the heart and the consequences are immense — it creates confusion around the choices we make. Feelings are the experiences of the heart and where our wisdom lies. To gain back clarity, we need to give our hearts back their rightful place and let go of the belief that we need to protect them. Instead, we need to accept that it is our hearts that will protect us. Feeling our deeper feelings is a natural, healthy, integrated and important way to understand where, and with whom, we share affinity. With whom we want to cultivate close relationships.

Cheryl Strayed wrote that: "NO is golden. NO is the kind of power the good witch wields. It's the way whole, healthy, emotionally evolved people manage to have relationships with jackasses while limiting the amount of jackass in their lives." Tuning into that quiet voice and learning to say NO is also the way we learn to affirm and refine who we want to be with. How we want to spend our time. Who we want to surround ourselves with. Whether it is our husband, wife, friend or the community we live within, we consider affinity. When we listen to our feelings, our affinity to certain people or experiences can guide us to understand the framework and relative location necessary for all to thrive.

Kahlil Gibran wrote of marriage:

On Marriage

You were born together, and together you shall be forevermore. You shall be together when the white wings of death scatter your days. Ay, you shall be together even in the silent memory of God. But let there be spaces in your togetherness, and let the winds of the heavens dance between you.

Love one another, but make not a bond of love: Let it rather be a moving sea between the shores of your souls. Fill each other's cup but drink not from one cup. Give one another of your bread but eat not from the same loaf.

Sing and dance together and be joyous, but let each one of you be alone, Even as the strings of a lute are alone though they quiver with the same music.

Give your hearts, but not into each other's keeping. For only the hand of Life can contain your hearts. And stand together yet not too near together: For the pillars of the temple stand apart, and the oak tree and the cypress grow not in each other's shadow.

Our bodies speak to us constantly, asking us always to align with our highest and wisest inclinations, sending feedback signals when things are out-of-balance or forced. Consider it is not about removing our defects or correcting our bent branches or smoothing out our rough surfaces as much as it's about developing a curiosity and an understanding for what it's like to be "you" in the world today. We do this so that we can experience a relationship with ourselves that is regenerative, forgiving and uplifting. So we can learn to be who we are meant and have the relationships with others that we wish to have. Learning to pay attention to our body's biofeedback loops and deepening our relationships with ourselves helps us clarify what kinds of relationships will work for us and in what proximity. Ideally, our closest relations exist in our lives in compatible ways for all, creating conditions for growth, support and benevolence towards each other. When we know which relationships and aspects of our lives mean the most, and which benefit from more closeness, including relationships within ourselves, we can apply the Permaculture's Zone philosophy to organize these relationships in our lives.

I believe making peace with our own imperfection is on the path to developing more compassion and tender-hearted bravery in our relationships. In Buddhism, they call this "maitri." Maitri is a Sanskrit word that speaks to the friendliness and benevolence we cultivate towards ourselves. As our practice deepens and becomes more habitual, we are better able to develop more sincere friendliness and benevolence, as well as understanding and compassion, for our relationships with people in our lives. As we deepen our practice of self-love and self-acceptance, we become better able to deepen our acceptance of others. We can better gauge the proximity in which we wish to engage with others, on what level and in what capacity. Because of the presence we cultivate in our bodies and our minds, we are able to more clearly recognize the presence of another and their place in our lives. The world becomes a colorful place and we get to choose who we want to play and learn with.

Developing a closeness and receptivity to our feelings, and responding appropriately to these feelings by recognizing which aspects of our lives cultivate kinship and which don't, both within the internal landscape and in the relationships we share with others, offers us guidance on how to apply this principle of relative location.

As we cultivate presence and relative location between and within ourselves, we are better equipped to stay with and deepen our relationships when challenges arise, both with ourselves and other people. It is also fair to say that sometimes, making peace with our imperfection as a means of deepening our own self-love and self-acceptance illuminates which relationships are creating struggle. This makes moving on easier.

Our thoughts and actions exist relative to each other, and we can design our lives, our thinking, and our actions just so, in the ways we need, so that we, as unique individuals, can exist in peace and remain open, instinctual and happy in the flow of our lives. Just as a Blue Jay drops acorns in a location that will eventually become an Oak canopy, which creates her future ancestors' habitat, we too can use relative location to create a synergy between our thoughts and actions to best serve our future needs. And our current needs, too.

It is because of our diverse intrinsic characteristics, our bent branches and rough edges — those very aspects of the self that make us imperfect and unique — that relationships form.

What does it mean to consider the relative location of our thoughts and actions as they relate to our lives, our circumstances and the lives of other people? How do we grow and reconcile despite our imperfections and learn to use them as gifts instead of perceiving them as obstacles?

We meet each other on the level that we are at. Like a chemical compound, when the vibration of the elements is different, each element will have to vibrate higher or faster or slow down in order to stabilize one and for the dynamic to maintain equilibrium.

All to say, we are free to exist in the world however best suits our needs. We are free to play and experience life and interact to the extent that we choose and that works for us. Some of us are introverted. Some are extroverted. Some of us find expression through the arts, some are inclined to reflect more methodically. Some of us are great listeners and others need to learn to listen more. It's a miracle and a testament to the human spirit that we cultivate meaningful relationships with people who are different from us. That we find ways of rounding each other out and supporting our differences in regenerative ways.

By understanding our priorities, we can assume a satisfying relative location for all of the treasured elements of our lives. Based on our personal needs, we can relate appropriately to other people and the intentions we have within those relationships. Relative location helps us understand how close we should be to elements in our lives, including other people. Permaculture's philosophy of Zones helps us organize and integrate those relationships within the whole of our lives, so that they reflect our values. As we begin to deepen our relationship to ourselves, considering the relative location of our thoughts and subsequent actions, it becomes easier to follow the path of least resistance within our lives. The more readily we consider ways to rearrange our lives and relationships, the more we maximize potential and growth for all in a sustainable and healthy way.

13

How to Start a Garden

ALL GARDEN CREATIONS START WITH A SITE ANALYSIS. We must assess the present conditions and strive to maintain a reasonable grasp of the obvious. Learn to recognize what is right in front of us. What does your garden look like now? Is it a barren yard with lots of wildflowers, weeds, odd artifacts, and misplaced "stuff" lying around? Does it reveal the natural landscape of who you are? It is tidy? Is it unkempt? Is it a magical garden that is grown and old with lots of nooks, or is it a desert oasis with curated structure? The same analysis applies to your life. Does it reflect your interests? What colors are present? What blocks exist? Are all elements thriving or are some thriving and others dying? If so, why?

We strive to observe and replicate natural patterns by creating functional connections amongst seemingly diverse elements. By developing the awareness to observe patterns in nature, including human nature, we are able to assess the essential aspects of all elements involved and understand how these elements best fit together. From here, everything is possible. From here, we can design.

So what's the best way to start a garden? To simply start.

You make the choice to create something meaningful and you identify the vision. Next, you cultivate an honest assessment of the present conditions and intrinsic qualities of the whole system by using core Permaculture principles (discussed in this book!). You review the landscape and identify existing problems. Initially, take care to not to get too attached to specific solutions. Remember, we want to arrive at design solutions, not impose them. Next, discuss the needs and available resources. Consider feedback loops between various elements on site, in the present moment, and assess how each contributes or detracts from the ideal experience. We affirm the vision and then start to draft our design.

Carl Jung said: "Where you stumble, therein lies your treasure." Bill Mollison was also quick to remind us that there are always seemingly insurmountable problems. How we perceive love, work, relationships, home, environment … all lays the groundwork for what we create. We need to clearly perceive where we are and where we want to be to chart a path forward. When we are aligned to the truth of our nature, we can see it all, we are in power. When we can see the patterns of our lives and observe, without judgment, where we are, we can begin to decipher our patterns of thought, word and deed. From there, we can make the necessary changes towards to craft a better aligned design for the internal landscape of our lives.

Absolutely nothing of great significance can be designed from a place of fear. The surest way to move beyond fear is to understand that fear is just a distraction that keeps us from seeing what is right in front of us. The remedy always grows alongside the poison. In nature, guilds, which are groups of species which use the same resources in similar ways, evolve naturally, over time, to curve each other out by diversifying certain functions within that guild. As we develop the practice of observation and interaction, we come to understand how elements function together, notice where problems exist, lean into them, and arrive at solutions that strengthen the integrity of the whole.

The only way to begin building what you dream — the proverbial garden of your life — is to start building now. Take small, repeatable, manageable steps you can build upon and replicate. When I create a garden, I don't think about past gardens. I may reflect on a past choice, or one I should have made, but all hands are on deck and my attention is fully invested in the project at hand. Full presence, full attention, full excitement, and full discipline are required to co-create the dream — the wild garden, the fulfilling and deep relationship you desire, a family, the career, the ideal financial set up. While it may be helpful to reflect on how things worked in the past, at this point, when you are ready to bring the dream out of the sky and allow it to set root, your vision and excitement become the talisman. These qualities, in honest alignment and calibrated relative location to your intention, anchor and guide the design process. To these qualities we return, over and over, we move forward along our paths and steward our visions to life.

14
Gardening
is Soil
Maintenance

*"If a healthy soil is full of death,
it is also full of life: worms, fungi,
microorganisms of all kinds ... Given
only the health of the soil, nothing
that dies is dead for very long."*

— Wendell Berry, *The Unsettling of America,* 1977

ALL GARDENING IS SOIL MAINTENANCE. Learning to understand soil is key for the aspiring gardener. Soil is everything. Without the right conditions, seeds will not germinate. Some plants have evolved over thousands of years to flourish in thick, clay soils, while others prefer sandy soil, and still others, rich and loamy forest soils. Some plants need to dry out in the hot sun to encourage the roots to grow and deepen, while others need constant moisture. Very often we try to force plants to grow in conditions they are not suited to, like the soil that naturally inhabits a particular home or climate or location but that is actually foreign to the plant.

If soil is the foundation from which all natural life germinates, consider then the foundation upon which you are building your life. What comprises the growing ground in your life? Consider your relationship to yourself, your relationship to your body, and your relationship to your environment. In this way, you can begin to understand where you "come from" and how you are working within the present conditions to best understand the makeup of what you wish to build your dreams upon. Engaging a creative curiosity for the environment within and without offers support and guidance to best prepare the foundations for new life to grow and flourish. How can you ensure your foundations are "nutrient rich"?

Very simply, when gardeners amend soil, we often add nutrients directly, like organic amendments rich in nitrogen, phosphorus and potassium, to encourage green growth, deeper roots, budding, blossoming, and absorption of other minerals. We strive to maintain a healthy pH for the desired palette, taking into account intrinsic characteristics. For example, the leaves of the oak tree fall to the ground to create acidic soil at the base of the tree. The acidic soil ensures that only plants suited to grow in the drip line of the oak's canopy can flourish and that they do not compete with the oak, or its tremendous root systems, for precious water.

To create balance, we consider adding or removing plants that sequester the appropriate minerals from the air and deliver them to the earth, feeding the root systems of other plants. We consider what organic matter is in the process of converting to compost. We want to create conditions for a healthy ecological guild and so prepare the soil to stack functions and support a plethora of life. We plant to encourage beneficial insects and birds, which come and feed from the plant and help build soil with manure, encouraging pollination and self-reliant, sustainable systems. In all cases, we seek to understand soil. What is the "come from" that creates the conditions for the next thing to happen?

As you prepare the soil in your life to plant seeds, you must understand the existing conditions and what life needs to flourish. Consider if your body, your environment, your thinking — the figurative soil present in your life — are just like the part you tend. Is anything too heavy? Too thick? Is there space for water and air to seep through? Are you affected by life, by other people, in healthy ways, or are you too self-contained? There are no wrong answers, in nature or in life, and an infinite number of solutions. Nature always seeks solutions and balance, so just observe how you move through the world and how your world exists in the moment.

Some of us have thick or heavy foundations. We root down and grow slowly, like many California natives or desert plants that have evolved to thrive in clay soil. Other plants push through cracks in the pavement. Some of us root down in spacious, fluid and fast moving environments, like the Amazon rainforest or New York City, breathing and moving in all directions at every moment. Life grows in all circumstances. We move in many ways.

You might ask yourself if the conditions within and without your personal life are, unlike clay, too loose. Are you metabolizing your experiences or are they draining too quickly? Do you have healthy boundaries, or are you overrun by people, taking on their feelings, thoughts and experiences as if they were your own? We can build substance from within by holding space for ourselves and our needs, increasing our sense of self and purpose in the world. If pumping up our soils with chemical compounds is akin to taking a steroid in the body to push a result, then organic gardening is akin to eating an apple every day, taking care of yourself and supplementing your body, your thoughts and emotions appropriately.

Whether your life's foundation is too heavy or too loose, the antidote is the same — compost. Compost is biomass, organic matter that has gone through a process of decomposition to produce a nutrient-rich soil amendment. It is, literally, organic remains of life that have broken down and changed forms to be useful in some other way. Compost can break up thick, clay soil so that air and nutrients can be absorbed more easily. Compost can also add substance and create cohesion in soils that are too loose and sandy.

The soil in your garden is like the soil in your heart. If your heart is closed, if your mind is closed, you are unable to absorb energy and nutrients from your environment, from your experiences. You are unable to decipher what is healthy and what is not — and to let what is healthy feed your soil and enable you to grow. You learn to create conditions in your life that allow you to integrate the "organic matter" of your experiences to enjoy, with full radiance, the life we all deserve. There is more than enough water for everyone. There is more than enough air for all. Create a compost pile of what you wish to keep, what serves you the most, and let it nurture you. Learn to swallow what you think you cannot and let it feed you. Learn to rest easy and trust you are experiencing joy, not by dumb luck, but because it is a reflection of the love you offer and of your true nature. Integrating our past experiences so that we can move forward and use them as messages, tools, medicines and salves is a useful practice.

If the soil of your being is too thick and you are stuck in your own impenetrable ways, it will be hard for you to open to new people, new ideas, to consider other ways in which the pieces of your life might fit together. It might then be hard to let go and allow life to unfold, to have trust in your world, to create space for life to happen naturally. In this one way, adding "organic matter" — in the form of people — might stimulate the soil of your life so that you can receive fresh air, absorb the minerals and nutrients from your present experience, and encourage new growth.

If your life lacks structure or substance, it's possible to suffer in the same way. Perhaps you are too easily swayed one way or the other, never really knowing where your personal "true north" resides, always out-sourcing your knowing and your power. Perhaps you are unable to really absorb what you need from your environment, your experiences, the people in your world, and to know then how to integrate and allow those experiences to assist you on your path. Building "organic matter" or the "compost" of your life can, in this case, add sustenance, substance and cohesion. Meaning it might then be possible, by integrating a deeper sense of purpose and self-worth, self-love into your life that you can then experience the people in your life more whole heartedly and in a more balanced way. You can offer more of yourself in a way that doesn't deplete you but that lifts you and everyone around you. You can come to know people in deeper ways that feed all to the core, not just superficially. Relationships build up from the bones, with equanimity and a more sustainable foundation of understanding and trust.

What does the compost of your life look like? Which experiences have you broken down and are now ready to reuse to feed energy to another part of your life? How might the compost of your life amend your soil, your foundation, your direction, and renew your sense of purpose?

Martha Graham wrote: "There is a vitality, a life-force, an energy and a quickening. And it is translated through you into action. And because there is only one of you in all of time, this expression is unique. If you block it, it will not exist. It is not your responsibility to determine how good it is or how valuable, or how it compares with other expressions. It is only your responsibility to keep it yours. To keep the channel open." Each one of us is complete-ly unique. We are each made up of many intrinsic characteristics, choices and patterns. Working with who we are, and making the necessary amendments in a uniquely curated way, is imperative so that we can live in the full expression of who we are meant to be. So that we can evolve as individuals and be of service to others during our time.

Learning how to approach life design from a natural, organic gardening perspective means taking a personal inventory of the present conditions, testing the soil, and then adding, or removing, to optimize the conditions. Only you know what you need. Only you know what feels right. For many people living in this culture, there is a tendency towards depression, anxiety and disconnection from nature, Mother Nature and our own human nature. Culturally, we find ourselves disconnected from our own true thoughts, our own strength, our own natural capacity for peace. Peace is not something we are ever going to experience because finally our lives are exactly the way we want them to look. The more we find peace in ourselves, the more we will find peace outside of ourselves. The more things fall into place. It's an inside job.

It is so very important to teach our children, and encourage ourselves, to digest each experience in life, the good and the bad. By managing the pace with which we absorb and integrate our experiences as individuals, families and communities, we can foster more balance and receptivity. As we stop and clear the clutter, as we make sense of what we are thinking and doing, we can improve the conditions of our lives. To grow strong, like trees, to build flexibility and grace and support from the roots, we need to set a personal foundation that is most appropriate for how we wish to grow. With a healthy foundation of support, an internal bed of balanced soil, we can more easily cultivate a direct relationship with ourselves. We can more easily digest each experience, knowing our future results from our present participation. If we wish to experience something new, we must be willing to look at who we are, how we contribute to what is occurring, and what lessons and blessings are present.

Only we know what is right for us. Only we know what we need to thrive. I have struggled with prioritizing what I think other people want or need me to be, or what other people think is right for me, outsourcing my own power. I am learning to listen to the quiet voice, the calm voice, the knowing deep inside. The more I listen, the more life rises to meet me and the more I am engaged and fulfilled. In this spirit of holistic design, we learn to listen and integrate all of ourselves. We find the connective tissue so that we can exist in the world with deep substance. From this place, we can repair our sense of disconnect, knowing that we are always inherently connected, We can begin to feel, act and move in concert with the world we live in. Life can be heaven or life can be hell. I've experienced it as both.

Sometimes getting your hands dirty, touching the ground, feeling the earth beneath your feet, taking stock of the smells, the tastes, allows us to lose our minds and come to our senses. Nader Khalili, the founder of the world-re-nowned earth-architecture institute, Cal Earth, often said: "Earth turns to gold." There are precious and integral systems at play in the soil. Humans used to be connected to the Earth. Our ancestors would walk barefoot or wear materials on their feet that easily conducted the Earth's energy, such as animal skins, and they would likely even sleep on the ground, at least part of the time. For much of humanity's existence, our lives were based on the natural rhythm of the seasons, and the daily rising and the setting of the sun. Because non-industrial humans lived so close to nature, their bodies were almost constantly infused with the energy of the Earth. You could say we were rooted. There was a firm connection.

In today's world, we are typically physically isolated from the Earth's energy. We live in insulated homes, often several stories above the ground. Our shoes are often made with rubber soles, which insulate us from the Earth's negative ions, and we travel around in motorized vehicles from place to place, isolating ourselves even further from the energy of Earth. And of course, as "developed and civilized human beings," we rarely ever sleep on the ground anymore. All things considered, it is likely that one of the few times that modern beings ever directly touch the Earth is if we are barefoot at the beach.

The Earth is continually giving off electrons and natural electrical fields, so that when we are directly in touch with such energy, our sympathetic and parasympathetic nervous systems are brought back into balance. This in turn supports a healthy immune system, proper circulation, synchronized biorhythms, and gives us a source of antioxidants that combat inflammation in our bodies.

Interacting in a visceral way with the natural world is a way of getting in touch with our own nature. Using our sense of taste, touch, smell, sight, and sound can connect us to the heart of our existence and can have a tremendously healing effect on all of us. It can help us remember that we are part of something really special, alive and much bigger than us. That the feelings of isolation or abandonment are just stories. They are not real. Putting our feet on the ground, practicing mindfulness, is a way of learning to be OK with life on life's terms.

As you begin to prepare the soil in your heart, consider what YOU need.

Consider the soil of your life. Learn to compost your experiences. Allow the unique expression of your life to naturally express itself. Tend your soil and watch your garden grow.

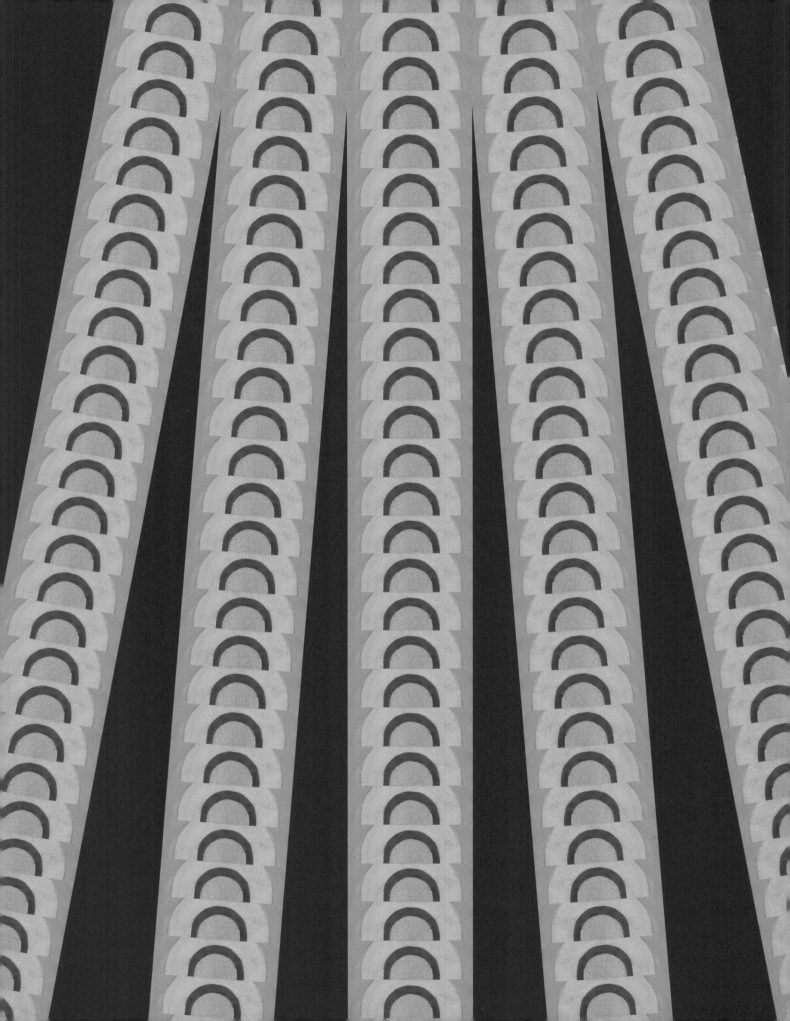

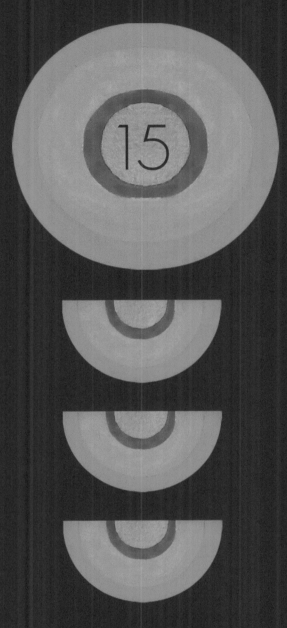

15

Seeds,

Roots

and

Fruits

CONSIDER HOW MUCH POTENTIAL IS PACKED IN A SEED. Consider all the stored energy that has been temporarily reduced to its essential components, just waiting for the right conditions to take root, to grow into its full expression.

Living from the bones, living from a place of heart, takes a lot of courage. It takes a lot of courage to ask yourself what you really want and to have the will to create the conditions your vision requires, completely and entirely, so the seeds you plant will grow. Every act of greatness starts with a simple intention. Each garden starts with just one seed.

The "planting seeds" metaphor has been used for hundreds of years; however, it is easy to overlook or downplay the miracle of germination. To hold an intention and plant that seed in the soil of our lives is the first step. From here, we must nurture the seeds we plant. We must create the conditions for life to happen, for our dreams to germinate. To think of all that goes on, unnoticed, beneath the soil, to germinate the life force of one seed and encourage a spring of life, is humbling.

So what does a seed need? Time. Time to break open, unfurl and set roots. There are nutrients, moisture, and darkness found beneath the soil and, with time, life incubates. Learning to trust the darkness of our lives is as essential as trusting the light. When we can close our eyes and still know where we stand we can find our balance. As we learn to trust what is unseen, we find the ground beneath our feet. When we can finally be OK within the particular conditions of our personal darkness, knowing that the world exists in a series of light and shadow, and that both are essential to growth, we have found freedom. How we learn to stay present with what scares us, what is unseen, what is beneath the surface of who we are, is the practice of tunneling, creating the conditions for life to germinate.

Seeds also need heat from the sun, from the light. Plant your seeds and shine a light on what you wish to grow. Shine a light from the best of who you are onto what you intend. Hold the best for what you plant and learn to interact with it in a non-polluted way. Learn to listen and speak from the heart without words. Give your seeds water, feed them what they need. And then practice patience as the process begins to take root and unfurl. Find the balance between light and darkness, rest and activity. This is how a garden grows. It is yoga, it is nature.

Planting seeds requires faith. Faith that you are held in the fabric of your life. Faith in the energy and time you have to create good, healthy, clear intentions. Faith in the necessary actions required to build a foundation of support. It is not your responsibility to figure out how it is going to look when the seed starts to grow, but to trust that they will. Your responsibility is to simply nurture, patiently and with care, what you have planted. To believe in the dreams you desire.

Trust is a big thing for a lot of people. If we cannot trust ourselves, we cannot trust others. When someone lies, for example, they then have to spend time creating more lies to keep the original lie intact. When we do the right thing, the right thing happens. When we don't, it doesn't. It's simple. The older I get, the more I trust myself. The more I trust my intuition and rely on my hard-earned wisdom for advice rather than the advice of others, the more patient I am knowing that it truly is a virtue.

We all must pay attention, daily, to what we have planted. Shine a light, daily, through mindfulness, on the seeds in the gardens of our lives. Shine a light by making love. Shine a light by refining our focus. Shine a light on what we love. Shine a light.

And then water the seeds in the ground. Just the right amount. Not so much that the seeds are inundated and float away. And not so little that the water evaporates. We water our gardens so that the soil can absorb moisture and soften the seeds. Let the soil soak up the heat of the day, let it settle. If our soil has been prepared, the right balance is easy to recognize, like a mother nurturing a child, like an artist giving birth to a great painting, or a musician writing a composition. We learn through practice and paying attention how much water our gardens need. We water our gardens by keeping our intentions alive. We water our gardens by making art. We water our gardens by expressing the emotions of our souls. Feel our feelings, listen to our hearts, let soften what needs softening and nurture what needs nurturing. When we feel what is real and alive, we water the seeds of happiness. Sing and we water the seeds of our dreams.

There is a wonderful Mayan story in "The Disobedience of the Daughter of the Sun" told by Martin Prechtel, a beautiful artist, writer, shaman and educator. The story explores the indigenous understanding of "the watery soul." This is the place where the heart of our love, our passions, our dreams, our feelings and our desires, reside. It is within the sea of our watery soul, beyond the thoughts and mental exercises we put ourselves through daily, that sound and vibration come together with something very primal, very much at the core of who we are — almost like an affirmation of our life force. Consider a bird. A bird does not sing because it has an answer. A bird sings because it has a song.

The feelings in our lives are energy in motion. They tell a story and they are meant to be felt. As we have discussed, we are not our emotions; we are so much more. However, within the sea of our emotions exist wonderful indicators, clues, suggestions, signposts of which direction to turn next. Of what we need to be in balance. Of what really inspires us, of what we love, of what we don't.

To feel an emotion is to water the seeds of our dreams by feeling what inspires us most, by feeling the joy, the sorrow, the humility and the ecstasy of being alive. To feel our emotions and water the seeds of our dreams, we affirm that our living, changing, moving, feeling, electrical bodies and souls are awake. Indeed, we can learn to feed our emotions back to the ground, back to this ever-receiving earth. It's one place that can handle the power of all our emotions.

We learn to sit with, to feel and to "let go," with great passion and intent, whatever arises. It is this act that purifies our bodies, frees us from the bondage of emotional insecurity. It is this act that frees the energy in our reserves so that we unleash our potential. Just like a seed, it is not about creating something that isn't there already, but it is about revealing what is waiting to exist — the joyful, vibrant, eccentric and entirely unique dreams that are our lives.

It is through this act of living with our emotions, of channeling our energy in productive, creative and life-affirming ways, that the seeds of our intentions begin to sprout to the surface and grow. From this point, roots begin to develop, leaves begin to grow, and the life of the plant begins to tell the story it was meant to tell. With all the power of the sequestered and harvested energy of its potential, and all of the intelligent impulses arranging, rearranging, bending and booming, shaped by its environment, it begins to grow.

One of the most poetic relationships in the natural world is between roots and fruits. The fruits of our labor, of our love, our passions and pursuits, are deeply integrated with the integrity and strength of our root systems.

There are three components that are key to healthy soil in a garden — nitrogen, phosphorus and potassium. Nitrogen encourages leaf growth. The leaves of a plant absorb nutrients from air, moisture, vitamins from the sun's rays. They are the nose, ears, eyes and skin of the plant. Phosphorus encourages root growth. Phosphorus helps the plant's roots grow down, while drawing nutrients and water from the soil up to through its branches to the tips. Potassium integrates the nutrients and helps the plant absorb the minerals it needs to stay healthy.

When we prune back a tree, say for example a fruit tree, the tree says to itself, "Oh no! I'm dying!" And it sends that energy back into the ground, to its roots, so that the roots will grow stronger, absorb more nutrients, absorb more water. It does this in its tireless and fearless commitment to live. And as the roots grow stronger, the plant grows stronger, and it then reaches a point of maximum capacity at which point it must send the energy back up its branches, to the light, encouraging more leaf growth, encouraging buds, blossoms. It does this because it wants to reproduce. And so the fruit tree begins to blossom, and is pollinated, and then its flowers become seeds, and the fruits begin to ripen.

You cannot expect a plant to bear fruit if you do not cut back what weighs it down and encourage the deepening of its roots. Like a fruit tree or flowering bush, we too need to cut back what weighs us down. We too need time to grow strong roots. We too need to allow ourselves the space to process and integrate our experiences, to absorb the nutrients of our surroundings and our practice, so that we may bud and blossom.

Not all trees bud and blossom at the same time and the world is filled with infinitely beautiful flowers. What does yours look like? What are the colors? The sounds? The smells?

"Lemon trees, they don't make a sound, until the branches bend and the fruit falls to the ground ..."
— Lucinda Williams

We all have gifts to give. We all have a unique flower that only our lives can create, a fruit that only our labor can bear. We have a lifetime to explore what we can nurture and give rise to in our gardens. We are seeds, born with an enormous amount of stored potential energy. Our dreams have buoyancy, our lives have power and our hearts have all the wisdom and energy we need to foster our dreams to fruition.

"Animals are something invented by plants to move seeds around. An extremely yang solution to a peculiar problem which they faced."

‑ Terence McKenna

16

Keep That Garden Growing

The key to helping a garden grow is attention. We learn to pay attention, with respectful curiosity, to how life evolves. We pay attention to how our gardens respond to various interactions and elements. Which plants thrive, which don't. We pay attention to the life in the leaves and the shapes that the leaves make in different conditions and at different times of day. We start to notice feedback loops. What needs more water, what needs less water, what needs assistance, what needs time. To maintain a garden, we follow these basic practices: pruning, weeding, feeding, mulching, harvesting, planting again. It's an endless cycle of rhythms.

When we begin to think about the art of pruning, it is important to understand this never-ending dynamic. Energy is neither created nor destroyed. Even a piece of paper that we burn becomes smoke and ashes. Things don't end. They simply change form. When we prune back a plant or a tree, we direct energy within the plant and the system to go where it's needed most. We encourage growth and strength in this way. We inspire shape. Similarly, in our lives, we can practice the art of pruning — deciding where we want to send energy within our lives and what we need to let go of.

We are so attached to the "stuff" we have accumulated that defines our lives, physically, emotionally and psychologically. We have an innate and biological fear of death and change. We have been taught to fear letting go. We have been taught to hold onto people, belongings, experiences, and memories, even when doing so comes at the expense of our own happiness.

When we finally discover that we are so much more than the stuff we hold onto, a tremendous opportunity arises. In fact, by releasing our attachments we create the conditions in our hearts to unleash our potential energy and allow it to find a new place in the world, in our lives, and in the ways we move through the world.

We often hold onto habits, people, ways of being in the world, and ideas about who we think we are that hold

us back from being the people we are meant to be. Life, nature — animals, birds, insects — are not concerned with how they move through the world or how what they "do" is thought of by others. They are, simply, in the flow. And because they flow in their lives, our lives are made possible. All these life systems — birds, bees, mycelium — do what they do so that we all can do what we do.

Learning the art of observation, of maintaining a reasonable grasp of the obvious, allows us to recognize, without judgment, what is serving us and what is not. As we practice regularly releasing what no longer serves the whole, we encourage our roots to grow stronger. We give new life to the buds and blossoms that await us, both in ourselves and in the world around us. Pruning gives us an opportunity to offer direction and create shape in our lives. The story is much more exciting than anything we can make up.

To keep our garden growing, we must also weed. Granted, the difference between a plant and a weed may be a judgment. Weeds are nothing more than misplaced plants. Perhaps we don't mind, and if so, let the weeds grow. They certainly have a place and function. They also can take water or nutrients away from plants that we want to grow. If so, we remove the weeds. As we begin to weed away what is distracting, blocking the view, or taking energy away from what we want to grow, we begin to reveal the structure and the form of our lives, our person.

A garden is a moving, living, breathing, changing organism. As life starts to take root, we are free to choose, again and again, along the way. We can pay attention and assist where possible, we can feed, we can prune, we can make choices, and then make new choices. It's a co-evolving relationship and we have the tremendous fortune of being one part of it.

This past spring, as the entire world went into lockdown to slow the spread of Covid-19, I walked through a garden we created with clients. I shared what I could about what we planted and relationships to the local ecosystems — the birds, the butterflies, the mountains beyond the fence line. We talked about how the plants will grow and mature in time, and what we can do to nurture their growth in the garden. As we walked under oak trees that were likely 200 years old, and have witnessed the passage of time in a way that is incomprehensible to humans, I was struck by a wave of calm and reprieve. Like so many, I have been feeling the ambient panic and dis-ease of a world without certainty that seems to be changing right before our eyes. I settled into the garden space and time seemed to slow. I began to notice the abundant new life sprouting, as rain had quenched the soil and root systems this past winter in California. I found myself enchanted, celebrating in a quiet way all the buds that were about to open, buds on plants we had put into the ground just one month earlier. I felt rejoiceful, grateful beyond measure for the consistency of nature's cycles. The spring buds, blooms, the blossoms to come, the change in light, the vibrant return of color within the landscape ... all a reminder of the season and cycles we are all a part of and move through together.

All gardening is Soil Maintenance. A thriving garden starts with a healthy foundation, healthy soil. A healthy body is the same. A healthy being has balance between Mind, Body, and Soul. I hope that as we make our way through this chapter of human history we find ways to strengthen and regenerate our social systems, that we explore together ways to strengthen our bodies through food and supplements, that we allow space for each of us to feel and find presence, and that we discover the real possibility of strong, healing and flexible relationships with ourselves, our communities and our world.

The Buddha has a million arms because there are a million ways to love. There are infinite opportunities and solutions available to us.

With a quiet mind and vibrant presence, we can reveal, maintain, nurture, and care for what is most essential to our lives. We quiet our minds so that we can learn to let it be. In doing so, the creative spirit has no option but to rise, like a phoenix, opening doors where we did not know they existed.

Be kind to yourself. Be kind to the planet. Be kind to the people in your life. As much as possible, and if possible, all the time. By growing a garden in our yards, in our hearts, in our lives, we discover that the most essential force we have with us, all the time, is love. Love it all as much as you can from where you are.

May your gardens flower wildly. May that surprise you, enlighten you, and show you things you have overlooked a hundred times or more. The miracle is really much more than what is seen. It is in the eyes that see.

"Is it not a magical thing, this life, when just a little ash, cinder, and unclear water can arrange themselves into a beautiful old woman who sways, lifts, kisses, loves, sickens, argues, loses, bears up under it all, and, wrinkling, still lives under all that and yet feeds the Holy in Nature by just the way she moves barefoot down a path?"

-Martin Prechtel, Unlikely Peace at Cuchumaquic

"That will be so amusing! You will have five hundred million little bells,

and I shall have five hundred million springs of fresh water..."

-Antoine de Saint-Exupéry, The Little Prince

Lessons Learned

It doesn't matter what you think or how you feel. It matters most what you do.

It's very hard to compete with someone's insecurities, including your own. Pay attention to the stories you tell yourself about yourself and others.

Be Brave.

What doesn't bend, breaks!

Bent twigs are beautiful.

Attachment is the rootlet of suffering.

There are many facets to who we are. Learn to recognize which part of yourself is steering the ship and choose wisely. Steward yourself and you steward the planet.

Listen to what people say AND do. Similarly, learn to listen to what people don't say and don't do.

When someone shows you who they are, believe them.

Don't let anyone rob you of your power, your joy, your freedom, or your sense of knowing what YOU need. No one can get the best of you unless you give it to them.

We are far more strong, resilient, courageous and utterly beautiful than we often give ourselves credit for.

Other people will reflect our power and our shadows to us. In all cases, compassion is an antidote.

Figure out where you are headed and take steps in that direction. If you are on the wrong path, it's never too late to make a change. Empower yourself with mindfulness and use your thoughts to cut through the fog of insecurity. Learn to be your own best friend.

Maintain a reasonable grasp of the obvious. Really think on this one. It can change your life. We often see life through the lens of our thoughts, not as it is. Practice seeing clearly what is being revealed.

There is a presence, not an absence, of life at all times. It is not about finding presence so much as getting rid of the stuff that inhibits your capacity to be present.

People are generally good and kind. I believe this. AND too, especially when up against their own stuff and the fear of facing themselves and their own shadows, people can be crude and selfish and insincere and manipulative and shallow and at the end of the day, it has nothing to do with you .

Don't take life personally.

Shine your light bright regardless.

((((What are you waiting for?))))

Be the person you want to spend your life with.

Give everything to your kids. It gives back a hundredfold. There are few things in life more rewarding than loving a child and nurturing them through each day. Children are miracles.

Buddhists suggest there are three accords - wake up, grow up and rise up. The latter two have less to do with knowledge and more with experience. Self knowledge is the gateway. Then being able to offer yourself to others is the challenge and the ultimate gift of being alive.

Remember - why should we let you live? What are you offering? What are you giving? What are you taking? You can tell a lot about the health of a society, or a person, by the trash they generate.

Everything has a consequence. Good, bad or otherwise.

Most of life occurs in the grey. People, experiences, life can be good AND bad. The non-duality of life is where the richness of knowing ourselves and others is found, as living, messy, beautifully imperfect beings.

How other people act towards you is much more a reflection of them than you.

Drink more water.

Your physical strength is a reflection of your mental strength and the two are forever intertwined and balanced by the other. Treat your body well, treat your mind well.

Learn to be self forgiving .

True love starts with self love. There is no way around it.

There is no sidestepping your healing. What you need to learn will find it's way to you so embrace it all.

Expect nothing, accept everything.

Learn to be a mirror of love for the people in your life, that they might hold that reflection and love themselves a bit more, too. We all need the encouragement.

Everyone has an opinion. What matters most is what is true to your heart. What drives you, what inspires you, what feeds you in the dark of night.

Be a steward to this earth. There is only one earth and it feeds us so greatly. Anything other than earth stewardship is greedy and cowardly. The seeds we sow are literally the ones we will reap.

Be a power of example to your children and others - be the change you want to see in YOUR world.

Let go of the past. There are always reasons why things ended the way they did. Why we make the choices we made. Accept them and move on.

If it seems weird it is. Stop wasting time trying to squint your eyes and tilt your head to make sense of things that don't resonate.

So much of life boils down to affinity. Let your faith win out over your fear and follow your bliss.

Love is truly the be all and the end all. There is absolutely no greater power in all of life.

Everything is relationship. Our bodies, our lives, our homes, our families, our friendships. We build guilds and determine, based on our relationship to the other, the world we inhabit. Nature is a supreme model for right relationship.

Weed your garden, tend the soil, sow the right seeds, discard what isn't bearing fruit and let it become something else. Your life is a garden.

Printed in the USA
CPSIA information can be obtained
at www.ICGtesting.com
LVHW072107141123
763627LV00004B/8